THE CAMPAIGN OF 1812

CASEMATE | ILLUSTRATED

THE CAMPAIGN OF 1812

Steven J. Rauch

CIS0054

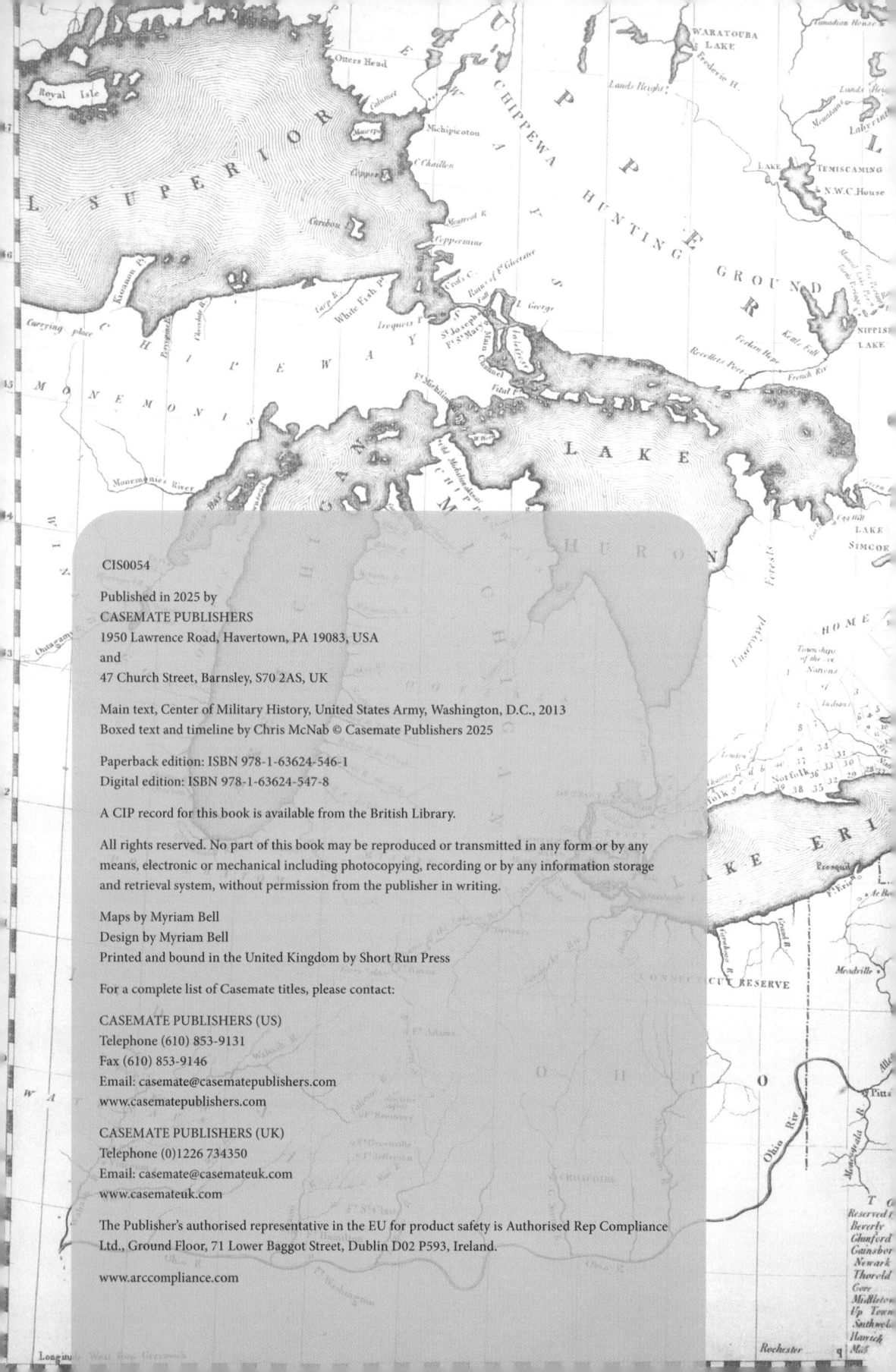

Published in 2025 by
CASEMATE PUBLISHERS
1950 Lawrence Road, Havertown, PA 19083, USA
and
47 Church Street, Barnsley, S70 2AS, UK

Main text, Center of Military History, United States Army, Washington, D.C., 2013
Boxed text and timeline by Chris McNab © Casemate Publishers 2025

Paperback edition: ISBN 978-1-63624-546-1
Digital edition: ISBN 978-1-63624-547-8

A CIP record for this book is available from the British Library.

All rights reserved. No part of this book may be reproduced or transmitted in any form or by any means, electronic or mechanical including photocopying, recording or by any information storage and retrieval system, without permission from the publisher in writing.

Maps by Myriam Bell
Design by Myriam Bell
Printed and bound in the United Kingdom by Short Run Press

For a complete list of Casemate titles, please contact:

CASEMATE PUBLISHERS (US)
Telephone (610) 853-9131
Fax (610) 853-9146
Email: casemate@casematepublishers.com
www.casematepublishers.com

CASEMATE PUBLISHERS (UK)
Telephone (0)1226 734350
Email: casemate@casemateuk.com
www.casemateuk.com

The Publisher's authorised representative in the EU for product safety is Authorised Rep Compliance Ltd., Ground Floor, 71 Lower Baggot Street, Dublin D02 P593, Ireland.

www.arccompliance.com

Contents

Timeline..................................6

Introduction..........................10

The U.S. Army in 1812.................13

British Forces in North America........19

U.S. Strategy.........................22

The Northwest Campaign and the
  Surrender of Detroit................26

The Frontier Besieged.................47

Disaster at the River Raisin..........57

War on the Niagara....................64

The Northern Theater..................80

Analysis..............................90

Further Reading.......................93

Index.................................95

Timeline

The War of 1812 was fought between the United States and Great Britain from 1812 to 1815. It was caused by a series of niggling tensions—British restrictions on American trade, the impressment of American sailors into the Royal Navy, and conflicts with American Indian tribes who were allied with Great Britain. The year 1812 saw some of the most brutal fighting of the war, with the Americans' three-pronged attack on Canada, prefaced by the battle of Fort Mackinac in July when a surprise British attack led to the surrender of the American garrison. On the Detroit Front in August, General Hull aimed to capture Upper Canada, but his army was forced to surrender, humiliated by General Brock and Chief Tecumseh. American morale plunged. In October, at the battle of Queenston Heights, an American attempt to invade Niagara was repulsed by Brock, though Brock lost his life in the battle. On the Montreal Front, American efforts to seize territory floundered because of poor coordination and supply lines. The year closed with a stalemate.

1812
Spring — Congress authorizes the president to ask the states to provide 30,000 federal volunteers for one year's service, the troops drawn from their militias. It also permits the president to call on the states to mobilize as many as 100,000 militiamen for up to six months.

March — Congress establishes the positions of quartermaster general and commissary general of purchases.

May — The U.S. legislature founds an Ordnance Department to develop weapons and equipment and to improve the condition of military stores.

Timeline

June 1 — The Northwestern Army begins its march on Detroit, seventeen days before Congress declares war.

June 17 — The United States invokes the war powers of the Constitution for the first time and declares war against Great Britain.

June 30 — Forces under Brigadier General William Hull reached the Maumee River Rapids and encamp. The army crosses the Maumee River the next day.

July 12 — Hull leads the invasion of Upper Canada.

July 17 — Following a landing on Mackinac Island, Michigan, British forces capture Fort Mackinac.

July 19 — New York militia under Brigadier General Jacob J. Brown repulse a British raid on Sackett's Harbor, New York.

August 7 — Following a series of tactical reversals, Hull orders his army to evacuate Canada.

▲ The painting *Surrender of Lord Cornwallis*, by John Trumbull, depicts the capitulation of the British Army at Yorktown, Virginia, in 1781. The end of the Revolutionary War began the haphazard growth of the U.S. Army. (DVIDS)

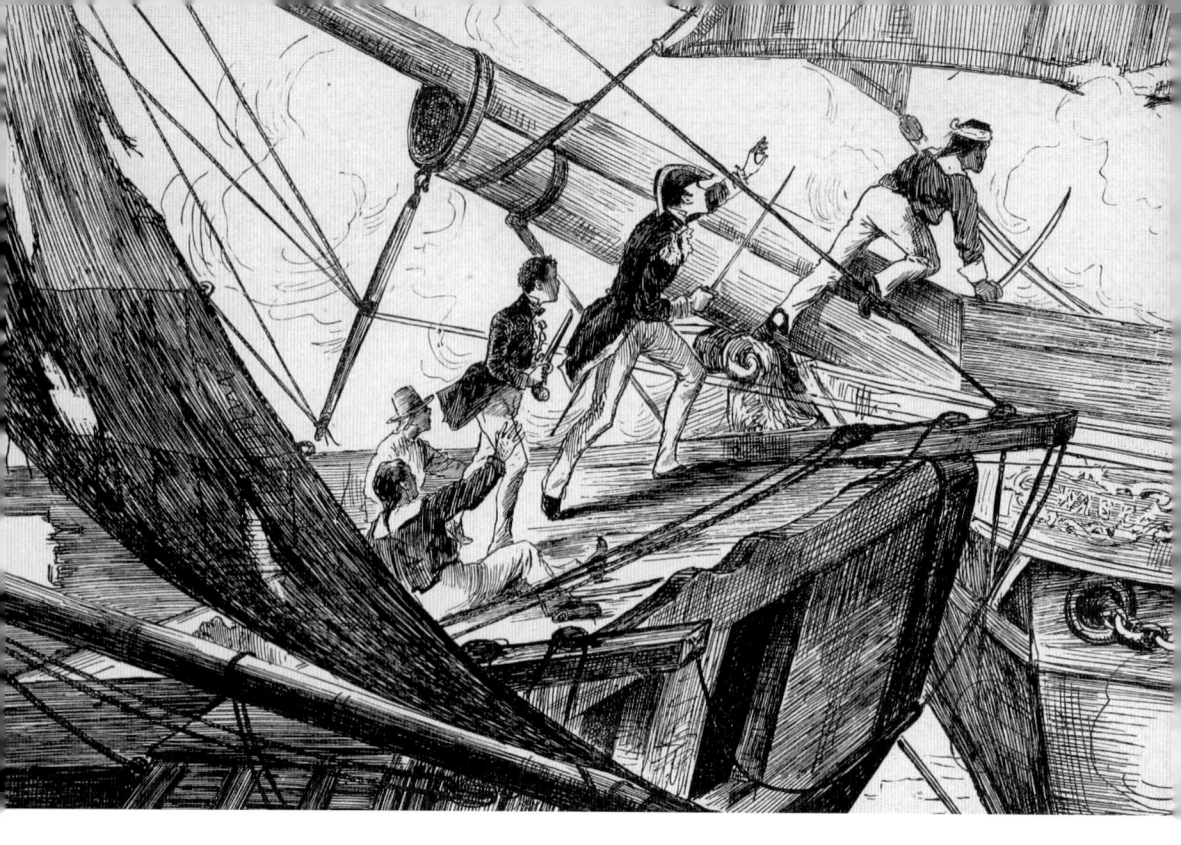

▲ In the 19th century, the lines between naval combat and land combat could be blurred, as sailors would be tasked with boarding enemy vessels and fighting the opposing mariners at close quarters with hand-held weapons. Here we see an American boarding party from the sloop USS *Wasp* assaulting the British brig *Frolic* on October 18, 1812. (*The Boys of 1812 and Other Naval Heroes*, 1887/Library of Congress)

August 9	Battle of Monguagon. U.S. troops are ambushed from British defensive positions near the Wyandot village of Maguaga, and are forced to retreat.
August 15	Battle of Fort Dearborn. A U.S. military and civilian column evacuating Fort Dearborn is attacked by four hundred Potawatomi warriors. The column is overwhelmed and fifty-three Americans are killed, most of them in a post-battle massacre.
August 15–16	Battle of Fort Detroit. A combined British and American Indian force under Major General Isaac Brock compels Brigadier General William Hull to surrender the fort and town of Detroit.
September	American Indian forces conduct multiple raids on U.S. outposts along the frontier territories.
September 24	William Henry Harrison is appointed as the commander of the Northwestern Army. Harrison plans to concentrate over four thousand troops at the Maumee River Rapids and advance to Detroit.
October 4	The British launch the first of several operations against Ogdensburg, New York.

Timeline

October 13 — Battle of Queenston Heights. U.S. regular and militia forces cross the Niagara River and assault British and Canadian troops at Queenston, Upper Canada. The attack is eventually contained and stopped by the British defenders, although General Brock is killed.

October 23 — Two hundred New York militia commanded by Major Guilford D. Young attack Akwesasne, a community of French-Catholic Mohawks, on the St. Lawrence River southwest of Montreal.

Mid November — Major General Henry Dearborn decides to undertake the long-awaited offensive to seize Montreal.

November 20 — Colonel Zebulon M. Pike crosses into Canada and with 950 men advances on Lacolle, a small village five miles north of the New York border. The British put up a brief defense, but are forced to retreat.

December 17 — A column of Kentucky cavalry, militia, and regulars from the 19th Infantry attack and burn a Miami American Indian town on the Mississinewa River in Indiana Territory.

1813
January 18–23 — First and second battles of Raisin River/Frenchtown. U.S. forces under Brigadier General James Winchester advance against a British and American Indian force at Frenchtown, south of Detroit. The British are initially ejected from the town on January 18, but a counterattack on January 22 defeated the Americans, who suffered more than 900 casualties.

February 22 — British commander Lieutenant Colonel George MacDonnell leads eight hundred men against Ogdensburg. The American defenders inflict heavy casualties on the attackers, but the village is eventually overrun.

Introduction

In June 1812, the United States invoked the war powers of the Constitution for the first time and declared war against Great Britain. The three-year conflict between the United States and Great Britain, known as the War of 1812, had its origins in periodic, yet persistent, confrontations between the two nations throughout the first decade of the 19th century.

▶ A portrait of Robert Stewart, Viscount Castlereagh, 2nd Marquess of Londonderry. Castlereagh served as the British secretary of state for foreign affairs from March 4, 1812 to August 12, 1822. (Sothebys/PD)

▼ *James Madison*, by John Vanderlyn. (White House Historical Association)

For many years, Great Britain had been embroiled in a desperate struggle against Napoleonic France. In its effort to cut France off from maritime trade, Britain had demonstrated little concern for the rights or sovereignty of neutral nations such as the United States. Unfortunately, the British blockade seriously damaged American trade and provoked constant friction on the seas. Britain's naval supremacy enabled it to seize American ships and take crew members believed to be Royal Navy deserters who had taken employment on American vessels. Britain did not recognize naturalized citizenship and enforced a doctrine that once a British subject, always a British subject. It is estimated that Britain impressed ten thousand Americans during its decades-long struggle against France. The repeated clashes over Britain's aggressive maritime policies and its support for American Indians hostile to the United States on the young nation's western and southern frontiers all contributed to the outbreak of war.

Introduction

The Campaign of 1812

Strategic Setting

Because the small size of the U.S. Navy precluded an effective naval response to British actions on the high seas, President James Madison decided to seize Canada as a way to obtain redress. Americans had several reasons to expect that a campaign against Canada would have a favorable outcome. The most obvious was that British military forces were fully engaged in fighting France and could divert minimal resources to North America. A second advantage was that U.S. forces would be close to their supply bases, while the British would be fighting an ocean away from home, further straining their already taxed logistical capability. The third advantage was demographic. The United States had a population around 7 million, while Canada's numbered nearly 500,000. Furthermore, many Canadians were of questionable loyalty, being of either French or American descent. Based on these considerations, many believed a U.S. victory was inevitable.

The U.S. Army in 1812

Whether the United States could fulfill its high expectations depended less on lofty aspirations than on the actual strength of its military forces, and here there were reasons for concern. In 1811, the U.S. Army consisted of a small corps of engineers; seven infantry regiments; and one regiment each of rifles, dragoons, artillery, and light artillery. The light artillery regiment was to be a mobile formation, but as a cost-saving measure, the government had sold its horses in 1808. The rest of the Army also suffered from a chronic manpower shortage, having just fifty-five hundred men under arms with another forty-five hundred positions vacant.

As the prospect for war grew imminent, Congress enacted several expansions. By June 1812, the authorized strength of the Army had grown to 35,603 men organized into twenty-five regiments of infantry, four of artillery (including the now remounted regiment of light artillery), two of dragoons, the rifle regiment, six companies of rangers, and various engineer and ordnance troops. In actuality, only 6,744 soldiers were on active service, scattered mostly in small detachments along the extensive frontier at such places as Fort Mackinac, on a small island at the straits of Lakes Michigan and Huron; Fort Dearborn, near present-day Chicago; and at trading centers such as Fort Osage, Missouri Territory, and Fort Hawkins, Georgia. In order to fill the ranks, the government offered a signing bonus of $16 for a five-year term of service, but few were willing to enlist for such a long time. Desperate to attract recruits, Congress reduced the length of service, added more financial incentives, and banned the practice of flogging. Despite all of these measures, the government failed to bring the desired number of men into the Regular Army.

One of the reasons that the Regular Army failed to draw recruits was that many men preferred the shorter enlistments and the attractive financial incentives

The Campaign of 1812

offered by their home state militias. The War Department estimated that 719,449 militiamen were available for active service. In the spring of 1812, Congress authorized the president to ask the states to provide 30,000 federal volunteers for one year's service drawn from their militias. It also permitted the president to call on the states to mobilize as many as 100,000 militiamen for up to six months of federal service. The numbers were impressive but deceiving, for most of the militia was poorly trained and equipped. Militia leadership was equally haphazard, with many state officers owing their rank to social status, political patronage, or popularity, as some units elected their officers. In short, the militia was a weak foundation upon which to base a national mobilization.

Issues of regionalism and politics also affected mobilization. The strongest support for the war came from those areas with the fewest resources to sustain it, namely, the South and the West. States in the Northeast were better situated for the conflict, but

▼ A collection of U.S. Army uniforms. Standard headgear for the common soldier was a "tombstone" shako cap with the unit insignia displayed on the cap plate. (U.S. Naval History and Heritage Command)

Profile: Fort Dearborn

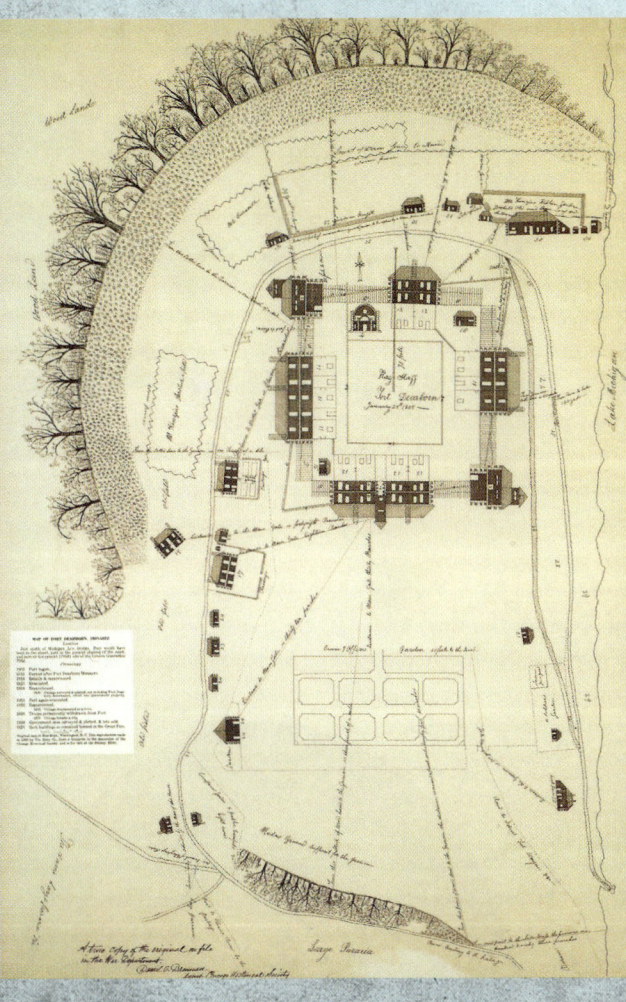

A map of Fort Dearborn, drawn in January 1808 by the fortress commandant, Captain John Whistler. The fort was burned after the battle there on August 15, 1812. (PD)

Fort Dearborn was first raised on the south bank of the Chicago River in 1803, a far-western outpost providing security for American trade and for military operations against hostile American Indians. It was named after the Revolutionary War hero and U.S. Secretary of War (1801–09) Henry Dearborn, and its construction was overseen by Captain John Whistler of the 1st U.S. Infantry. The outer perimeter of the fort consisted of a twelve-foot-high wooden stockade, guarded at the northwest and southeast corners by two elevated blockhouses. To the east, Lake Michigan provided a further natural defense, although woodland surrounding the remaining arc of the fortress gave covered fields of approach for enemy warriors. Between 1803 and 1808, the fort was substantially developed. Its facilities came to include not only the soldiers' barracks, officers' quarters, and the commandant's quarters, but also a hospital and a magazine. Reporting in 1812, a contemporary commentator remarked that "this fort was remarkably well calculated to hold out against Indians—lying in the bend of a deep river and nearly surrounded by it; built of very substantial materials, with two rows of high pickets and two Block houses which guarded every point including the communication between the Lake and Chicago River." The fort was, however, vulnerable to concerted attack, and was taken and burned to the ground by an American Indian force in August 1812. A second fort was built on the site in 1816, but it was decommissioned in 1840 and finally removed in 1856.

The Campaign of 1812

their support was less than wholehearted. When Republican President Madison issued his call for militia, several of the New England states, where the Federalist Party was strong, refused to supply troops on the grounds that Madison's intended purpose did not meet the missions authorized in Article 1, Section 8, of the United States Constitution "to execute the Laws of the Union, suppress insurrections, and repel invasions." Some state courts ruled that the federal government did not have the authority to require militia to cross international borders to fight outside the United States, reserving that decision exclusively to the commander of a state's militia. As a result of these legal challenges, the federal government would experience difficulty in raising militia forces from the Northeast throughout much of the war.

Getting men into the ranks was only the start of the government's problems. Feeding, equipping, training, and moving the Army likewise posed daunting obstacles, particularly given the rudimentary transportation network that existed along the frontier with Canada. Nor did the Army have the bureaucratic infrastructure to wrestle with the burgeoning issues of mobilizing and sustaining a wartime force. In 1812, the entire War Department consisted of Secretary of War William Eustis and eight clerks. Eustis had been a surgeon during the Revolutionary War and was later elected to the House of Representatives. President Thomas Jefferson had appointed him secretary of war in 1809 because he was a staunch member of the Republican Party. His military and bureaucratic skills were limited.

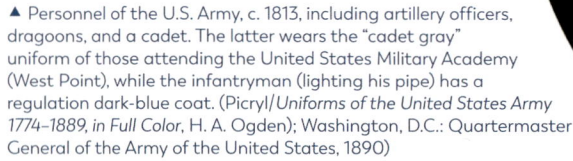

▲ Personnel of the U.S. Army, c. 1813, including artillery officers, dragoons, and a cadet. The latter wears the "cadet gray" uniform of those attending the United States Military Academy (West Point), while the infantryman (lighting his pipe) has a regulation dark-blue coat. (Picryl/*Uniforms of the United States Army 1774–1889, in Full Color*, H. A. Ogden); Washington, D.C.: Quartermaster General of the Army of the United States, 1890)

▶ William Eustis, by Walter M. Brackett. (U.S. Army Art Collection)

The U.S. Army in 1812

In March 1812, Congress attempted to rectify some of the Army's administrative deficiencies by establishing the positions of quartermaster general and commissary general of purchases. Then in May, the legislature created an Ordnance Department to develop weapons and equipment and to address the deplorable condition of military stores. As many as one in five of the Army's weapons were inoperable, and much of its ammunition had been procured in 1795. Shortages of everything from tents and shoes to medicine and other items likewise existed. Unfortunately, without central direction, the quartermaster general, commissary general, chief of ordnance, and various contractors would often compete for the same resources, adding further chaos to the Army's primitive logistical system.

The Army's senior officer in 1812, Major General Henry Dearborn, had a stellar record of service during the Revolutionary War, serving in all major battles in the northern theater, including Bunker Hill, Saratoga, Monmouth, and Yorktown. He had aligned himself with the Republican Party, and when Jefferson had become president in 1801, he had appointed Dearborn as secretary of war. Dearborn, who had served in that office until Eustis replaced him in March 1809, had been thoroughly involved during his tenure with reducing Army force structure under Jefferson's Military Peace Establishment Act of 1802. Although considered the nominal commander of the U.S. Army, Dearborn lacked the statutory authority and the staff to fully oversee Army operations, and, like Eustis, he was overwhelmed by the crush of responsibilities incumbent with mobilizing and guiding the national war effort.

▼ U.S. Navy uniforms of the War of 1812. The officer on the left has the pattern of uniform established in 1802, revised in 1813. Clothing for common sailors was highly variable, as there were no formal uniform regulations for the lower ranks. (U.S. Naval History and Heritage Command)

The Campaign of 1812

As for the officer corps, it was as unprepared for what lay ahead as the rest of American military establishment. If most militia and volunteer officers were rank amateurs who owed their posts to their political and social connections, then the officers of the Regular Army were not much better. The nation's small Regular Army was a backwater in American society that did not necessarily attract the finest talent, while the Jefferson and Madison administrations had often applied a political litmus test in selecting officers. A glimmer of professionalism existed among a few individuals, but these were the exceptions to the rule. Perhaps the Army's best hope for the future, the U.S. Military Academy at West Point, New York, was by 1812 barely ten years old and had produced just 120 graduates, of whom 99 would serve in the war, mostly in junior positions. As for the rest, one of the nation's more gifted military leaders, Lieutenant Colonel Winfield Scott, claimed that the older officers had "very generally sunk into either sloth, ignorance, or habits of intemperate drinking," while the new officers were for the most part "course and ignorant men ... swaggerers ... decayed gentlemen, and others—'fit for nothing else,' which always turned out utterly unfit for any military purpose whatever."

▲ *Henry Dearborn*, by Walter M. Brackett. (U.S. Army Art Collection)

British Forces in North America

Opposing the United States was one of the strongest military and economic powers in the world. The British Army had nearly one hundred thousand men in service in 1812 and could draw replacements and reinforcements from a population of 18 million. Most of Britain's resources were tied up in the war against Napoleon, so for the time being, very little assistance could be spared for the defense of Canada.

In 1812, there were about fifty-five hundred British regulars in Canada, with about twelve hundred of those in Upper Canada (present-day Ontario). Backing them were contingents of Canadian militia who, much as their American counterparts, were of questionable effectiveness. During the war, the provinces of Upper and Lower Canada would provide about ten thousand militiamen.

Lieutenant General Sir George Prevost served as the captain general and governor in chief of British North America, an office that combined both civil and military functions. Prevost had entered the army in 1784 and distinguished himself as a competent leader. In 1808 he was promoted to lieutenant general, and in 1811 he became the governor of British North America. As war loomed, he judiciously managed his limited resources by improving the state of the Canadian militia and by raising several provincial units for long-term service. More importantly, he protected the vital rivers and lakes that formed his lines of communications and support by improving fortifications and by constructing armed vessels. Prevost initially feared the United States would attack either Montreal or Quebec, so he concentrated his slim forces for the defense of those points. He wanted to avoid decisive engagements with the Americans and hoped the war would be solved through diplomatic means before military action could begin.

Profile:
Major General Sir Isaac Brock (1769–1812)

Isaac Brock is a legendary figure in Canadian history, lauded as the "Hero of Upper Canada" for his ultimately mortal service during the War of 1812. He was born on October 6, 1769, in St. Peter Port on the island of Guernsey, England. He moved around as a child, living in Southampton and the Netherlands. But in 1785, the teenage Brock bought a commission to enter the British Army as an ensign in the 8th (King's) Regiment of Foot, transferring to the 49th Regiment in 1791. Brock demonstrated all the diplomatic and moral qualities of a leader, and in 1797 he became the regiment's commanding officer (as a lieutenant colonel). In 1802 he was posted to Canada, where he attained the ranks of colonel in 1805 and major general in 1811, taking command of all British troops in Upper Canada. Also in 1811, he was appointed the president of the Executive Council of Upper Canada, thereby becoming Upper Canada's civil governor as well as its military leader.

The War of 1812 made Brock's reputation. His defeat of Major General William Hull at Fort Detroit in August 1812 demonstrated both his intelligence and his daring; for this action, he was awarded a knighthood of the Order of the Bath. Brock was developing a reputation as a master of the calculated risk, but at the battle of Queenston Heights on October 13, 1812, he personally overreached, being shot and killed while launching an impetuous attack, although he helped secure the overall victory that day.

▲ Isaac Brock. (Public domain)

Major General Isaac Brock assisted Prevost as lieutenant governor and military commander of Upper Canada. He had been a soldier since he was sixteen years old and commanded a regiment at twenty-eight. When he arrived in Canada in 1802, he found an army with low morale, poor discipline, inadequate supplies, and strained relations with the citizens. Brock's dominating personality enabled him to resolve many of the problems. The British soldiers soon realized they could expect strict but fair treatment from him and discipline soon improved. After ten years in Canada, Brock had become thoroughly familiar with the people, the geography, and his responsibilities.

The British hoped to offset their limited manpower through an alliance with the American Indian nations residing in

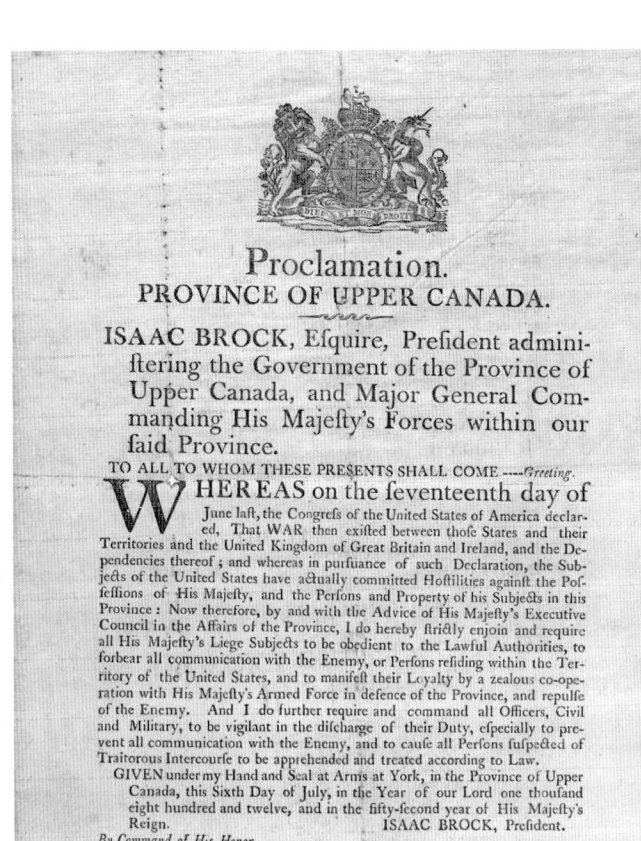

British Forces in North America

Upper Canada and adjoining U.S. territories. The most influential American Indian leader was Tecumseh, a Shawnee who had fought the Americans at the battle of Fallen Timbers in 1794. In the years leading up to the war, Tecumseh and his brother Tenskwatawa, known as the Prophet, had attempted to form a confederacy of American Indian nations to oppose further American settlement in the Northwest. The Prophet preached a return to American Indian values and the renunciation of white civilization. The brothers believed that land belonged to all American Indians in common and could not be ceded by individual tribes in treaties with America without the consent of all the nations. During the War of 1812, many American Indians supported the British war aim of attaining an independent American Indian buffer state in order to halt further American incursion into the Northwest Territory. The British welcomed Tecumseh's leadership and determination to fight in an alliance against their common enemy.

◄ A proclamation by Isaac Brock, the administrator of Upper Canada, on July 6, 1812, announcing the declaration of war by the United States against the United Kingdom, and requiring the residents of Upper Canada to be obedient to the British authorities and to cooperate with the British armed forces in defense of the territory. (Library and Archives Canada/Bibliothèque et Archives Canada)

◄ Color version of Benson J. Lossing's portrait of Tecumseh. (Public domain, Toronto Public Library)

U.S. Strategy

The initial U.S. military strategy was relatively simple. The U.S. Army would invade and conquer Canada, while the U.S. Navy would take to the seas to harass British commercial shipping. An offensive to seize Montreal via Lake Champlain and the Richelieu River offered the shortest route into the most vital part of the enemy's territory. The capture of Montreal would cut British lines of communications along the St. Lawrence River to Upper Canada, thus severing at one stroke British control of everything to the west, including Lakes Erie and Ontario. President Madison favored this approach, since it would simplify logistical support. Unfortunately, the U.S. Army was scattered along a vast frontier from the Great Lakes to New Orleans and to concentrate it in one location would take time and expose American settlements to British or American Indian attacks. The most immediate forces available to seize Montreal were the militias of the northeastern states. However, as New England and parts of New York were the centers of Federalist opposition to the war, little support for such an offensive could be expected.

Given the above calculus, General Dearborn proposed that the United States invade Canada at three points simultaneously. In the Northwest, an army at Detroit in Michigan Territory would invade western Upper Canada to disrupt British influence with the American Indians and deny the British access to the upper Great Lakes. A central offensive would be aimed at Upper Canada in the Niagara River region to cut access between Lakes Erie and Ontario and to suppress any American Indian involvement on that frontier. Finally, a northeastern offensive into Lower Canada would be aimed at cutting the St. Lawrence River between Lake Ontario and Montreal, with the capture of Montreal being the ultimate objective. Dearborn believed this three-pronged strategy would so stretch Prevost's limited resources that he would be unable to oppose the advancing columns effectively at all points. Dearborn's strategy of multiple operations along an extensive and remote frontier required the ability to synchronize operations so as to bring resources to bear simultaneously at all points. If on the other hand the operations were to occur sequentially, the British might

◄ The naval clash between the frigate USS *Essex*, led by Master Commander David Porter, and the British sloop HMS *Alert* on August 13, 1812, resulted in the first capture of a British ship in the War of 1812. (*American Naval Battles*, 1837, via Internet Book Archive/PD)

The Campaign of 1812

Notices.

Two water communications are open for the passage of troops to Mahinak — one by the way of Lake Huron, and the other by way of the Ouisconsing. The upper part of the Illinois River is too shallow, in summer and autumn, to admit the passage of Boats. Troops may move from St Louis, by way of the Ouisconsing, to Mahinak, in 35 or 40 days. They can receive provisions at St Louis to last them to Prairie des Chiens, and at that place they can procure provisions to last them to Mahinak. Provisions may likewise be obtained at the mouth of Fox River on Green Bay.

The distance from Detroit to Mahinak is between 5 and 6 hundred miles — and the lakes may be navigated either by Vessels, or open Boats — the latter must follow the sinuosities of the shore.

If we have command of the straits of Detroit, and the water as far as Lake St Claire, the British in Canada can have no communication with Mahinak, except by way of Grand and French Rivers — the latter of which enters Lake Huron. Trading Boats pass this route, from Montreal to the straits of St Maries, in 12 days — so says an English writer on Canada — and the probability is, that troops may perform the same route in 20 or 25 days. By placing a sufficient Garrison on, or near the mouth of French River, no supplies can be sent to the troops above — of course they must soon perish from want, or abandon their positions.

Perhaps it may not be difficult to possess ourselves of Fort St Joseph in the straits of St Maries — it is

▲ A letter from Major Amos Stoddard to Secretary of War William Eustis, dated August 20, 1812. It contains logistical information to accompany another text, entitled "Outlines of a plan for an attack on Canada." (NARA)

◂ John Randolph had a successful political career from 1799 until 1830, serving in the U.S. House of Representatives and the U.S. Senate. He was one of those voices vigorously opposed to the U.S. declaration of war in 1812. (National Portrait Gallery)

be able to shift their forces to defeat each column individually. Furthermore, only by controlling the Great Lakes and its adjacent waterways would the United States be able to easily project, sustain, and communicate with its military spearheads. Unfortunately, the United States did not possess a naval organization on the Great Lakes with which to control those vital waterways. As a result, supplying forces in remote theaters, such as Detroit or northern New York, would present a complex logistics problem for which no one in the War Department had any previous experience. In short, General Dearborn's grand plan stood on shaky legs. Furthermore, once he had submitted it, Dearborn left the task of coordinating the three American armies to Eustis, and concerned himself only with the army under his personal command in the Northeast.

The Northwest Campaign and the Surrender of Detroit

Although intended to be a coordinated effort in which U.S. forces advanced against Canada on three fronts simultaneously, the westernmost American army moved first, alone and unsupported. The Michigan Territory held strategic importance because it bordered on the northwest American Indian nations and the western section of Upper Canada. The territory had a population of about forty-seven hundred white inhabitants, many of French descent, living near Detroit and the western shore of Lake Erie south to the Maumee River Rapids, at present-day Toledo, Ohio. In 1812, the territory was ill-prepared for war, protected by a small militia battalion, one company of the 1st U.S. Infantry commanded by Captain John Whistler, and a detachment of the Corps of U.S. Artillery with twenty-three artillery pieces at Fort Detroit (see Map 1).

▼ *William Hull*, by Gilbert Stuart. (National Portrait Gallery)

In the spring of 1812, the War Department decided to improve the military situation by raising a force in Ohio, designated the Northwestern Army, and by sending it to Detroit where it would be available in the event of war. Normally the most expedient way to travel to Detroit was via Lake Erie to the Detroit River. However, since the United States did not possess the naval forces to protect water transportation, the Northwestern Army had to march overland through a wilderness into a logistically austere theater of operations.

Map 1

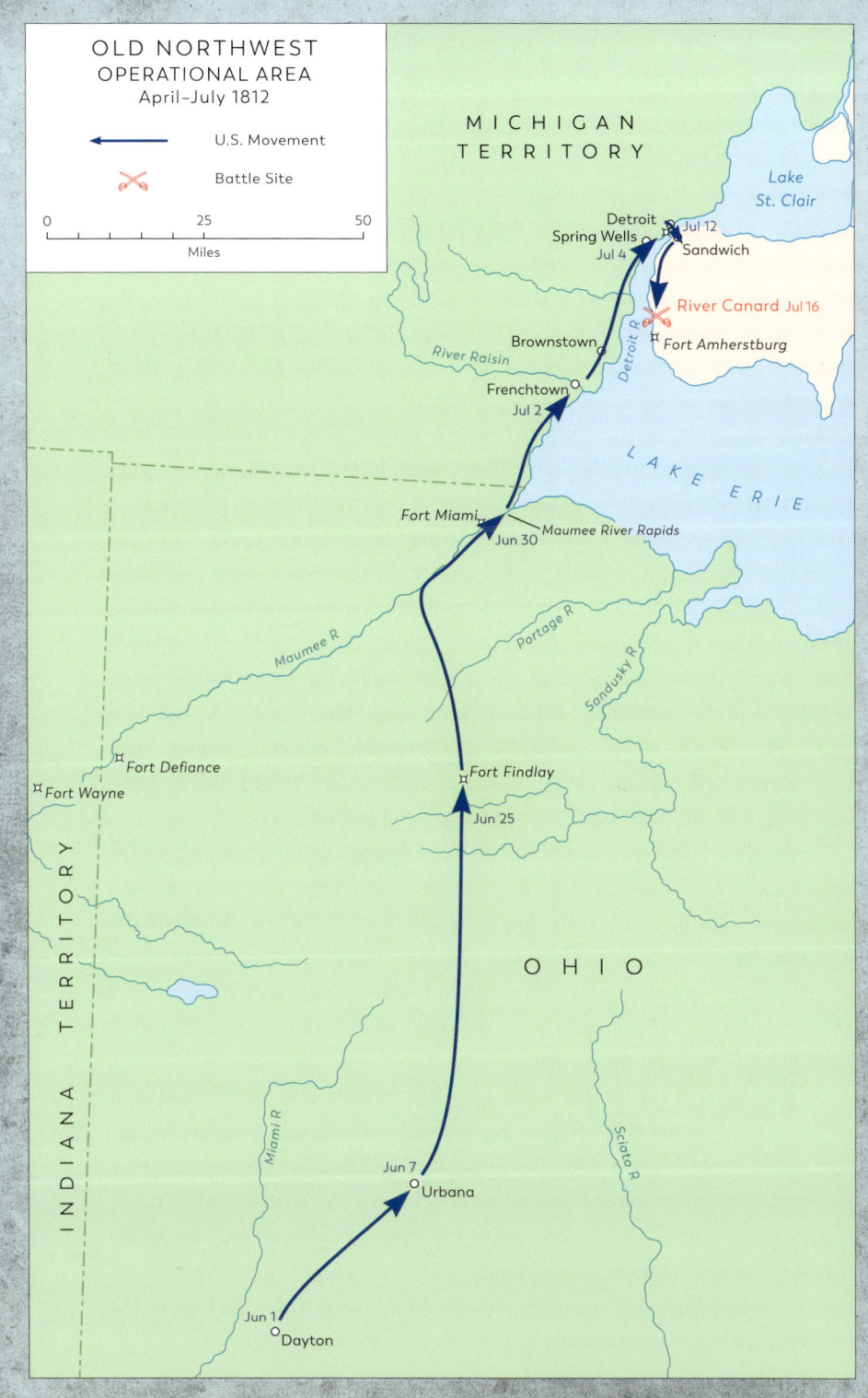

The Campaign of 1812

President Madison asked Revolutionary War veteran William Hull to command the Northwestern Army. Hull had a firm grasp of the military situation and cautioned Eustis and Madison about the challenges of invading Canada. In a letter to Eustis on March 6, 1812, Hull stated that the British held the strategic and tactical advantage in resources and geographic position. His greatest fear was from the American Indians, particularly those living along the western shore of Lake Erie astride his line of communications between Detroit and Ohio. Hull believed the situation could be improved only if sufficient effort was made to gain control of the Great Lakes through an ambitious shipbuilding program. Unable to influence Eustis or Madison of the risks involved in their plans, he agreed to try to accomplish the mission without naval support.

Madison's orders to Hull included several specific tasks. First, Hull had to provide security to the Michigan Territory. Next, in the event of war, he would invade Upper Canada to remove British influence over the American Indians. Last, Hull was to take control of Lake Erie bordering Canada and cooperate with any other U.S. forces sent to operate in that theater. To accomplish these objectives, Secretary of War Eustis asked Governor Return Jonathan Meigs of Ohio to provide 1,200 volunteers from his state militia. Meigs appointed Duncan McArthur, James Findlay, and Lewis Cass, none of whom had significant military experience, as colonels of the regiments, each comprising about 400 to 500 men. Hull also received the veterans of Tippecanoe, 275 men of the 4th U.S. Infantry commanded by Lieutenant Colonel James Miller, stationed at Vincennes. In addition, he had a light cavalry troop and a detachment of rangers and scouts.

The militiamen rendezvoused at Dayton, Ohio, during April and May and quickly demonstrated how little experience they had with military life. Their weapons were in such poor condition that Army Quartermaster James Taylor organized artificers with a traveling forge to repair their weapons on the march. Before the army began its march, Hull sent out scouts who reported that the American Indians and the British were aware of his preparations. The absence of operational security would plague Hull throughout the campaign.

The geography of the theater dictated in large measure how the Northwestern Army could move and be sustained. The territory was vast, with primitive forests, deep swamps, marshes, and rivers. It was sparsely populated, with an average of only six persons per square mile in a band of territory seventy-five miles along the fringes of the frontier. This lack of settlement meant that the army had to depend on supplies obtained hundreds of miles away in southern Ohio or western Pennsylvania. After supplies were stockpiled at magazines, usually at the last town near the frontier, the problem then became transporting them to the army in a timely manner.

The Northwestern Army began its march for Detroit on June 1, seventeen days before Congress declared war. At Urbana, Ohio, the 4th U.S. Infantry joined the

The Northwest Campaign and the Surrender of Detroit

column. The militia's dislike of military discipline became manifest during an incident in which the men of one company refused to march any farther until they were paid. Hull ordered some regulars to use their bayonets to prod the recalcitrant unit along. The stern demeanor of the regulars was sufficient to induce the militiamen to march, whereby Hull told Miller, "By God, sir, your regiment is a powerful argument. Without it I could not march these volunteers to Detroit."

As it moved, the army cut a crude road through the heavily forested country. The militia regiments provided the pioneers, who worked ahead of the main army cutting a path fifteen to twenty feet wide through heavy timber. As with most nineteenth-century armies, the Northwestern Army carried a great deal of impedimenta, requiring one hundred twenty teams of horses. The army's wagons carried fourteen thousand pounds of flour and drovers herded three hundred head of cattle for food. Adding to the logistical burden were the many servants, wives, children, contractors, and other civilians who followed the army.

To secure and extend his supply line, Hull's men built blockhouses every twenty miles or so to serve as magazines for storing and issuing supplies. This preparation was necessary since the column was moving almost two hundred miles beyond cultivated areas and thus could not count on obtaining forage along the route. Hull garrisoned these posts with sick and invalid soldiers, a process that so reduced his force that he wrote to Eustis asking for more militiamen to protect his line of communications.

▼ Reenactors smartly portray soldiers of the U.S. Army 3d Infantry Regiment (The Old Guard), which served in Upper Canada during the War of 1812. (DVIDS/U.S. Army Alfredo Barraza/Released)

The Campaign of 1812

Poor weather, accidents, and injuries also hindered the march. Constant rain created mud that mired wagons and caused horses to drop dead from exhaustion. Despite these difficulties, the army still managed to advance an average nine and a half miles per day. By the time the army reached Fort Findlay on June 25, the baggage wagons could not keep pace. The horses were tired, and forage was so scarce that the food allowance for the horses and oxen had to be reduced. To add to the challenges, Hull received constant dispatches from Eustis urging him to reach Detroit as soon as possible.

While the Americans were conducting this movement, the British were not idle. The main base for British operations in the region was Fort Amherstburg, on the southeast bank of the Detroit River, where it commanded the waterway used to travel to Detroit. Lieutenant Colonel Thomas B. St. George commanded the garrison, which numbered about three hundred regulars of the 41st Foot and Royal Newfoundland Infantry Fencibles. In addition, he had about eight hundred fifty militia and four hundred American Indians from various tribes. The militiamen were of uncertain loyalty because many were American expatriates, or related to U.S. citizens. Adding to Fort Amherstburg's strategic significance was the fact that it was a major naval construction yard, producing such vessels as the gun brig *General Hunter*, the sloop-of-war *Queen Charlotte*, and the schooner *Lady Prevost*. The fort also hosted the headquarters of the British Indian Department, which had responsibility for coordinating diplomatic, military, and economic relations with regional American Indians, as well as providing annual gifts of food, clothing, and weapons. U.S. officials saw Fort Amherstburg as a major obstacle to American control of the Northwest.

As the Northwestern Army advanced, Hull's scouts reported large American Indian encampments near Brownstown, Michigan Territory, and Fort Amherstburg. On June 30, Hull reached the Maumee River Rapids and encamped near the Fallen Timbers battlefield, the scene of General Anthony Wayne's victory over the American Indians on August 20, 1794. The army crossed the Maumee River the next day by fording and by boat.

In order to comply with Eustis's prodding to get to Detroit quickly, General Hull arranged for the small, unarmed schooner *Cuyahoga* to take medical supplies, the sick, and some officers' wives to Detroit via water. Someone placed Hull's official papers on the vessel, including the army's muster rolls and his correspondence with the secretary of war. On July 1, *Cuyahoga* sailed north into the Detroit River and past the guns of Fort Amherstburg. St. George had received notice on June 30 that war had been declared, so he sent a small gunboat to capture *Cuyahoga*. Hull's correspondence, which gave complete insight into the American operation, proved an intelligence coup.

On July 2, as his army neared Frenchtown, Michigan Territory, on the River Raisin (present-day Monroe, Michigan), General Hull received a dispatch from Secretary of War Eustis notifying him that Congress had declared war on June 18. Unfortunately, Eustis had sent the notice through the U.S. postal system instead of using a special courier, which resulted in a significant delay in this important information reaching Hull. Upon arriving at Spring Wells, three miles south of Detroit, Hull heard cannon fire as the guns of Fort Detroit attempted to sink the British warship *Queen Charlotte* in retaliation for its capturing *Cuyahoga*.

◀ Remnants of a military corduroy road near present Brownstown Charter Township, Michigan, near the mouth of the Huron River on Lake Erie. This type of road was built of logs, placed side by side, to form a traversable road over low or swampy areas. (Andrew Jameson/CC-SA 3.0, via Wikimedia Commons)

The Campaign of 1812

When the army reached Detroit, Hull attempted to procure food and forage. Eustis had directed a civilian contractor, Augustus Porter, to provide three hundred sixty-six thousand rations for Hull's army. However, Porter failed to deliver the provisions, citing the inability to move them by water. The army also needed medical supplies since these stores had been captured aboard *Cuyahoga*, and none were available in Detroit. Resupply could only reach the army by the road it had just cut from Ohio. On July 9, Hull requested Eustis to supply the army with two hundred thousand rations of beef and flour, and assistance to secure his line of communications; otherwise he feared, "this army will perish for want of provisions."

In the meantime, new orders arrived from Eustis directing Hull to "take possession of Malden [Fort Amherstburg], Upper Canada, and extend your conquests as circumstances may justify." Hull replied to Eustis that he would cross the river into Canada but warned, "The British command the water and the savages; I do not think the force here equal to the reduction of Amherstburg; you therefore must not be too sanguine."

Hull was not aware of the British situation on the other side of the river, which was in great confusion. The British had been trying desperately to improve the defenses of Fort Amherstburg. Witnesses described the Canadian militiamen as mutinous with a desire to desert as soon as the American army crossed the river. St.

▼ A view of the soldiers' barracks area of Fort Mackinac on Mackinac Island, Michigan. The Americans unsuccessfully tried to reclaim the island in July–August 1814. (ID 175752736 © Gerald D. Tang/Dreamstime.com)

The Northwest Campaign and the Surrender of Detroit

A map of the Detroit region during the War of 1812, showing the location of key battles and skirmishes. Detroit itself quickly surrendered to the British in 1812, but was taken back by U.S. forces in September 1813. (Kevin1776/CC BY-SA 4.0, via Wikimedia Commons)

George's lack of confidence in the militia led him to evacuate Sandwich (present-day Windsor, Canada) and concentrate his forces south at Fort Amherstburg.

Meanwhile, Hull experienced his own problems with the militia. One Ohio company from Colonel McArthur's militia regiment refused to enter Canada, claiming that it could not be required to fight outside the United States. The militiamen also exercised little fire discipline and accidentally wounded a major from Colonel Cass's regiment. Nevertheless, Hull initiated the invasion of Canada early on July 12. Colonel Cass's Ohio militia and Colonel Miller's 4th U.S. Infantry regiments embarked from Detroit aboard small boats and landed north of Sandwich fifteen minutes later. After McArthur's regiment landed, Hull sent it out to forage supplies for the army. The expedition returned after four days with considerable quantities of flour, whiskey, and salt.

On July 13, Hull issued a proclamation urging Canadians not to resist. He warned against their collaboration with the American Indians stating, "No white man found fighting by the side of an Indian will be taken prisoner. Instant destruction will be his lot." The proclamation had the desired effect. Almost six hundred Canadian militiamen at Fort Amherstburg deserted and returned home to their families and crops.

The Campaign of 1812

▶ A map of Upper and Lower Canada in 1812. Even the most cursory glance at the map tells the viewer much about the strategic importance of lakes and rivers in the theater. (Map by Thomas Kensett, via Wikimedia Commons/PD)

The Northwest Campaign and the Surrender of Detroit

▲ The shores of Mackinac Island near what is appropriately called British Landing. It was here that the British, Canadian, and American Indian forces landed on July 16–17, 1812. (ID 42273082 © Smontgom65/Dreamstime.com)

On July 16, Hull ordered Cass to reconnoiter enemy positions near a bridge on the River Canard, a deep stream that connected to the Detroit River about four miles north of the British fort. The British had stationed a small picket of men near the bridge. The picket opened fire as the Americans approached. Cass endeavored to flank the position, but the marshy terrain forced his unit to march three miles east to a ford where it crossed to the south bank of the river. The British detected the flanking movement and withdrew, abandoning the bridge to the Americans. During the skirmish, one British soldier was killed and another captured.

Cass sent a message to Hull requesting permission to hold the position. Hull was concerned about having a small detachment beyond supporting distance from the main army and within range of enemy naval gunfire from *Queen Charlotte*, so he ordered Cass to return. Cass complied only after a council of officers insisted that he follow Hull's orders. Following two days of inconclusive skirmishing, Hull's subordinate commanders began to suspect that the general was afraid of confronting the enemy. But Hull's experience during the Revolutionary War had taught him that proper preparations had to be made to ensure the favorable outcome of a siege. On July 21, the general wrote to Eustis explaining that an attack on Fort Amherstburg without artillery would result in a great sacrifice of men.

Meanwhile, over three hundred miles to the north, British forces seized Fort Mackinac. The fort guarded the straits connecting Lakes Michigan and Huron, supported the fur trade, and served as a symbol of American power to the American Indians. American Lieutenant Porter Hanks commanded the post with sixty-one men and several 9-pounder cannon. British Captain Charles

The Northwest Campaign and the Surrender of Detroit

Roberts on St. Joseph Island had decided to capture Fort Mackinac with a mixed force of British regulars, Canadian fur traders, and several hundred American Indians. On July 16, this force of over six hundred men embarked on boats for their objective forty miles away. At about 0300 on July 17, Roberts's force landed and moved two 6-pounder cannon to a hill overlooking Fort Mackinac. Hanks did not know that war had been declared and at dawn discovered Roberts's men with their artillery aimed at his position. To avoid a massacre, he surrendered the fort. Roberts paroled the Americans and sent them in a boat to Detroit.

As word about the British victory at Mackinac spread, American Indian tribes that had been vacillating about their allegiance decided to assist the British cause. Meanwhile, logistical problems consumed Hull. On July 31, he received intelligence that the Wyandot American Indians south of Detroit at Brownstown had joined the British and would attempt to interdict American supplies sent overland from Ohio. Unaware of Hull's predicament, Governor Meigs had already dispatched Captain Henry Brush with a supply train that included a herd of cattle and barrels of flour to resupply the army at Detroit. Brush made it only as far as Frenchtown, about fifty miles south of Detroit, before the Wyandot blocked further progress.

Hull dispatched two hundred militia commanded by Major Thomas Van Horne to meet and escort the convoy to Detroit. Van Horne's expedition began on

▼ A summery view across the Fort St. Joseph National Historic Site, Ontario, overlooking Lake Huron. It was used as a staging post for the British attack on Fort Mackinac in July 1812. (D. Gordon E. Robertson/CC BY-SA 3.0, via Wikimedia Commons)

The Campaign of 1812

August 4 and reached the Ecorse River about eight miles south of Detroit where it encamped for the night. Tecumseh meanwhile had established an ambush with twenty-four American Indians in the thick woods along the road at Brownstown. Early the next day when Van Horne's force moved into the ambuscade, Tecumseh and his men attacked. The surprised militiamen thought they faced a superior force and quickly retreated. The American Indians killed seventeen soldiers and captured two during the short fight. They scalped the dead Americans, skewered them with stakes, and left the bodies along the road to deter future attempts. Concerned about the interdiction of his line of communications to Ohio, on August 7 Hull ordered his army to evacuate Canada.

Once back at Detroit, General Hull ordered Colonel Miller to assemble a 600-man force of the 4th Infantry, some militia, and two pieces of artillery to make another attempt to reach the convoy waiting at Frenchtown. Meanwhile, the British decided to send one hundred fifty men of the 41st Regiment of Foot, fifty militia, and about two hundred of Tecumseh's American Indians to stop the Americans. The British crossed the Detroit River on August 8 and established their blocking position near the village of Monguagon (now Trenton, Michigan). In late afternoon on August 9, the lead elements of Miller's force came under fire from the enemy ambush. Miller quickly formed his men into line, fired a

▼ Unlikely allies Tecumseh and General Isaac Brock looking down on Detroit, awaiting the return of messengers, dispatched to General Hull, with a demand for surrender. (Public domain, via Wikimedia Commons)

Map 2

The Campaign of 1812

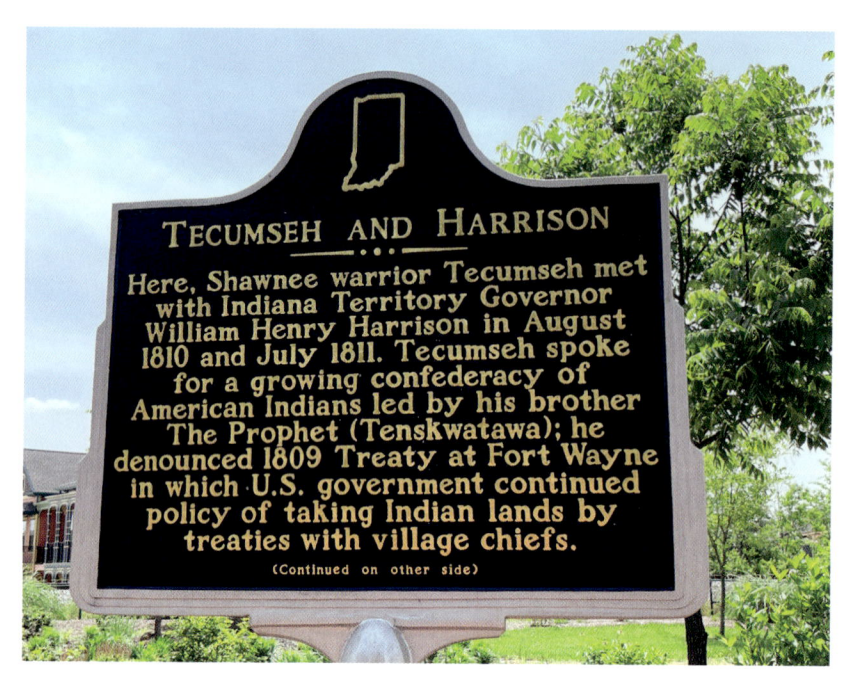

◀ A historical marker at Grouseland—the home of William Henry Harrison during his tenure as the first governor of the Indiana Territory—in Vincennes, Indiana, explains the pre-war meetings between Harrison and Tecumseh. (Riis2602/CC BY-SA 4.0, via Wikimedia Commons)

massed volley, and advanced on the enemy with bayonets. One witness, Major James Dalliba, recalled, "The incessant firing in the centre ran diverging to the flanks; from the crackling of individual pieces it changed to alternate volleys; and at length to one continued sound; and while everything seemed hushed amidst the wavering roll, the discharge of the six-pounder burst upon the ear. The Americans stood!" The battle of Monguagon lasted a little over two hours, during which time the British lost six killed and twenty-one wounded and the Americans eighteen killed and sixty-three wounded. Having lost almost 13 percent of his force, Miller believed he could not advance any farther, and he requested help from Hull to transport the injured back to Detroit. Three days later the exhausted men, the cream of Hull's army, returned to Detroit because they were not able to link up with the supply train.

Isolated and low on supplies, Hull desperately needed the rest of the U.S. Army to reduce the pressure on his beleaguered force by attacking other points of the British defensive system, just as envisioned in American strategy. It was not to be. Believing that he needed more time to prepare for his advance from New York into Canada, General Dearborn, without consulting Madison, Eustis, or Hull, agreed to a truce proposed by British General Prevost. The truce, which did not include the Detroit area, went into effect on August 9, the same day as Monguagon. In one stroke, Dearborn had undercut his own strategy of breaking the British by placing simultaneous pressure on several points of their overextended line. Upon learning of the truce, President Madison wrote to Dearborn on August 9:

The Northwest Campaign and the Surrender of Detroit

Eyewitness: Battle of Fort Dearborn

The following report of the battle of Fort Dearborn, and its subsequent massacre, is from the diary of one Charles Atkins, who received the information directly from Captain Heald (here spelled "Heel"). The text is largely given in its original form, without editing:

Sept. 22, 1812. In consequence of orders from Governor Hull to Capt. Heel [Heald] commanding officer at Chicago everything was given to the Indians that was in the Garrison even provissions—and all the Garrison with the Women and children left that place to march through the Woods to Detroit in the morng of their departure he had information that the Indians meant to attack but having no provission left they were obliged to persevere in their determination of going to Detroit, after leaving the Garrison and going about one mile Capt. Wells rode forward a little and found the Indians about 500 in number hid behind some sand banks and other places, he immediately returned to Capt. Heel and advised him to charge the Indians with his company, which was Done in a Gallant manner as they had to ascend a small sand bank the Indians took advantage of it and fired on them. They killed half of his men, his men then fired and killed 6 Indians. He then advanced and drove the Indians after which he gaind a small height and formed his men on it, here he had a commang situation, he had then but 29 men left, 19 of these wounded. A half Indian was sent to him to say that if they would give up they would be taken treated as prisoners, situated as he was obliged to capitulate—his Wife was with the baggage where all the Women and children were killed, 12 Children in one Waggon were butchered, Mrs. Heel after receiving 5 Wounds was saved by Mr Jno Burnet.

It was much to have been desired that simultaneous invasions of Canada at several points ... might have secured the great object of bringing all Upper Canada ... under our command. This systematic operation having been frustrated, it only remains to pursue the course that will diminish the disappointment as much as possible.

Dearborn responded on August 15, writing that he did not realize that he was to synchronize his operations with Hull, and that he did not even know he was to take the offensive against the eastern portions of Upper Canada along the Niagara and St. Lawrence Rivers. As he told the president, "No explicit orders have been received by me in relation to Upper Canada, until it was too late, even to make an effectual diversion in favour of Genl. Hull."

Meanwhile, on August 13, Hull decided to make another attempt to reopen his supply line. He ordered Cass and McArthur with four hundred of the fittest militiamen to link up with the waiting supply convoy by traveling along a circuitous American Indian trail to the River Raisin. The two colonels were not eager to undertake the expedition. Unbeknownst to Hull, they had written to Governor Meigs urging him to send two thousand men to help them. After Hull repeated his order to the colonels, they finally departed late in the evening. Once they left Detroit, they failed to keep Hull informed of their location (see Map 2).

The Campaign of 1812

The Northwest Campaign and the Surrender of Detroit

Realizing that the fall of Fort Mackinac and his own predicament at Detroit had rendered the frontier vulnerable, General Hull ordered Captain Nathan Heald at Fort Dearborn (present-day Chicago) to evacuate that post and move the garrison along with its dependents east to Fort Wayne, Indiana Territory. Before the evacuation could be implemented, hostile Potawatomi warriors gathered around the small post. To assuage their threats, Heald offered them clothing and other goods in exchange for a promise not to interfere with the evacuation, whose security was somewhat improved by the arrival of U.S. American Indian agent Captain William Wells and some reinforcements. About midmorning on August 15, the column departed Fort Dearborn and moved along the south shore of Lake Michigan. The soldiers and their families had traveled less than two miles when four hundred Potawatomi attacked them. Heald immediately led a counterattack and a fierce melee ensued. Some American Indians made their way to the baggage train where they attacked the women and children, a few of whom fought back with swords and muskets, including Heald's wife, Rebecca. The American Indians demanded Heald surrender and he agreed if they promised there would be no further slaughter. After granting these terms, the warriors reneged and began to kill the wounded Americans. The massacre resulted in the deaths of twenty-six regulars, all of the militia, two women, and twelve children, for a total of fifty-three Americans. Among the dead was Lieutenant George Ronan, the first West Point graduate to be killed in combat.

On the same day that Potawatomi warriors massacred Heald's column, General Brock demanded that Hull surrender Detroit. Hull was shocked to learn that the British commander of Upper Canada was at Detroit. He had assumed that Brock was still in the East fending off the planned American offensives against the Niagara and St. Lawrence Rivers. Brock, however, was far better informed about American operations than Hull, and he had used his control over the waterways to rapidly transfer three hundred men to Detroit. Moreover, unlike Hull, Brock knew that Cass and McArthur were not far away and that he needed to resolve the situation at Detroit quickly before they could intervene. Consequently, Brock put on a demonstration designed to make Hull think that he had more men than he actually had and added a threat to his ultimatum, warning that if Hull did not surrender, Brock's American Indian allies "will be beyond my control the moment the contest commences." Demoralized yet defiant, Hull rejected Brock's demand that he surrender, stating that it was his duty to fight and "accept any consequences which may result."

Immediately after receiving Hull's rejection, Brock ordered his artillery to fire on Fort Detroit from the Canadian side of the Detroit River, and soon two British warships joined in. An eyewitness account of the terrible effect of the British cannonade is provided by an officer's wife who wrote:

◀ Henry Herring's sculpture "Defense" features on the wall of the southwest tower on Michigan Avenue Bridge, Chicago, Illinois. It shows the clash between soldiers and American Indians around Fort Dearborn, 1812. (Paul R. Burley, CC BY-SA 4.0, via Wikimedia Commons)

> A 24 pound shot entered the next door ... and cut two officers who were standing in the entry directly in two their bowels gushing out, the same ball passed through the wall into a room where a number of people were and took the legs of one man off and the flesh of the thigh of another.

One of the men killed was the unfortunate Lieutenant Hanks. This event further undermined the morale of the troops and civilians who had sought refuge in the fort. Early in the morning of August 16, under covering fire from the guns of *Queen Charlotte* and *General Hunter*, Brock led his army across the Detroit River and surrounded the fort. At this point, Hull determined he had three alternatives. He could accept a fight in the open, endure a siege, or surrender. As to the first option, Hull estimated that only about eight hundred of his twenty-five hundred men were healthy and available for battle due to disease, casualties, desertion, detachments, and the dispatch of Cass and McArthur's four hundred soldiers whose status was unknown to him. Brock had about fifteen hundred American Indians, soldiers, and militiamen, although he made the force appear larger to the Americans by lighting additional campfires and parading his men back and forth in view of the fort. Given the apparent odds, Hull decided it was unwise to do battle outside the fort.

▲ *Surrender of Hull's Army at Fort Detroit*, by Henry Louis Stephens. (Library and Archives Canada)

As for the second option, Hull wrote Eustis that Fort Detroit was crowded with women, children, and "the old and decrepit people of the town and country." Supplies were short, and Hull believed the fort could only be sustained for a few days. Moreover, the British cannonade and Brock's threats had already impressed upon Hull the suffering this course of action would impose on soldier and civilian alike.

The third alternative—surrender—seemed the only viable one. Hull chose this option out of "a sense of duty and full conviction of its expediency." On August 16,

Profile:
Brigadier General William Hull (1753–1825)

▲ General William Hull rose through the officer ranks during the Revolutionary War and was lauded by George Washington, although he is more often remembered for surrendering Fort Detroit to General Isaac Brock on August 16, 1812. (New York Public Library)

William Hull's story is one of rise and fall, the latter being the most extreme professional descent. He was born on June 24, 1753, in Derby, Connecticut. He later studied law at Yale College, where he became a close friend of Nathan Hale, who distinguished himself as a soldier and spy during the Revolutionary War. After practicing law for some years, Hull served as an officer in the Continental Army, leading men into action at the battles of White Plains, Trenton, Princeton, Saratoga, and Monmouth. Hull proved to be a capable and respected commander, and attained the rank of lieutenant colonel by war's end. He resigned from the army and returned to law, serving as a judge to the General Court of Massachusetts. In 1805, however, President Jefferson appointed Hull as governor of the Michigan Territory. As war with Britain became imminent, Madison offered Hull a commission as a brigadier general to command U.S. forces in the region. Hull at first declined the appointment, but after an alternate commander became ill, he reluctantly accepted the command on April 3, 1812.

Hull's service in the War of 1812, and his subsequent legacy, was defined by a series of failures. His leadership of the invasion of Canada was poor and chaotic, invasion turning into retreat. His surrender of Fort Detroit with no effective resistance to the British and American Indian allies on August 16, 1812—despite his enemy having far fewer troops—was deemed so egregious that he was court-martialed and sentenced to death, only saved by a pardon (but not exculpation) from President Madison. The war cost him much: his own son, Abraham, was killed at the battle of Lundy's Lane on July 25, 1814. Hull subsequently retired from professional life, working on his defensive memoirs until his death in 1825.

The Campaign of 1812

A peaceful depiction of Fort Mackinac. Initially in U.S. hands, the fort was the site of one of the early battles of the War of 1812, and it was soon captured by the British. (PD, via Wikimedia Commons)

the Americans marched to the parade ground and stacked their arms while the British cut the American flag from the staff and hoisted the Union Jack to the accompaniment of "God Save the King." Under the terms of capitulation, Brock pledged to protect the inhabitants of Detroit from the American Indians and allowed the American militiamen to return home on the promise that they would not take up arms again. Hull and over five hundred eighty regulars became prisoners and were sent to Quebec for internment. The surrender of Detroit was catastrophic for the United States. In less than three months, the Northwestern Army had been eliminated and the United States had lost the strategic Fort Detroit. Public opinion and the Madison administration blamed General Hull for the failure. After his release from captivity, Hull was tried by court-martial in 1814 for treason, cowardice, neglect of duty, and unofficer-like conduct. With none other than General Dearborn serving as president of the court, Cass, McArthur, and other officers, all since promoted, gave the primary testimony against Hull. During the trial, Hull sarcastically stated, "If it all arises out of their achievements while under my command, I must say, that it appears to me my expedition was more prolific of promotion than any other unsuccessful military enterprize I ever heard of." On March 26, 1814, the court acquitted Hull of treason but convicted him on all the other charges. The court recommended that he be sentenced to death but that the sentence be commuted in light of his service during the Revolutionary War. On April 24, Madison approved the findings and recommendations of the court and remitted the punishment. Hull was dishonorably discharged and his name removed from the rolls of the Army.

The Frontier Besieged

British victories at forts Mackinac, Dearborn, and Detroit encouraged the American Indians of the Northwest to attack American settlements throughout the Indiana, Illinois, and Iowa territories. On September 3, a war party of about twenty Shawnee, Delaware, and Potawatomi American Indians descended on the small frontier community of Pigeon Roost, Indiana Territory, about one hundred miles south of present-day Indianapolis. Moving from cabin to cabin, they killed two men, five women, and sixteen children in an hour and then burned down the empty homes. The next day, one hundred fifty militiamen set out to find the American Indians, but they were not able to do so.

▼ Henry Bathurst, the 3rd Earl Bathurst, was the British secretary of state for war and the colonies between 1812 and 1837. His strategic leadership during the War of 1812 was largely neglected on account of his focus upon the European theater of war. (National Portrait Gallery/PD)

The next attack occurred on September 4 at Fort Harrison, Indiana Territory, a stockade fort on the Wabash River north of modern Terre Haute and named for former territorial governor William Henry Harrison. There, a large force of Kickapoo, Miami, Potawatomi, Shawnee, and Winnebago warriors laid siege to the post. Captain Zachary Taylor commanded the fort with a company of sixty soldiers of the 7th U.S. Infantry. During the eleven-day siege, the American Indians burned a hole in a portion of the palisade, but Taylor and his men improvised repairs and repelled the assault. For this victory during a summer fraught with U.S. military defeats, Taylor achieved fame and a brevet promotion to the rank of major.

The raids, however, did not stop. On September 5, bands of Sauk, Fox, and Winnebago American Indians led by Black

Hawk attacked at Fort Madison on the upper Mississippi River in what is now the state of Iowa. The garrison avoided defeat when the American Indians ran low on ammunition, which enabled the soldiers to escape using a trench dug from one of the blockhouses to boats moored on the river. Simultaneous with the attack on Fort Madison was an assault on Fort Wayne, Indiana Territory, perhaps the most important remaining post in the northwestern theater. Fort Wayne had four cannon and a garrison of seventy soldiers commanded by Captain James Rhea. On September 5, bands of hostile American Indians began attacking the settlers near the fort. During the next week, Rhea and the garrison repelled repeated attacks.

When word arrived in Kentucky of the siege of Fort Wayne, William Henry Harrison sprang into action. Harrison was the 39-year-old son of Benjamin Harrison III, a signer of the Declaration of Independence. William Harrison had joined the Army in 1791 and had served on the frontier under Major General Anthony Wayne, from whom he had learned the importance of logistical planning, rigorous training, and firm discipline. After participating in Wayne's victory over the Ohio American Indians in the 1794 battle of Fallen Timbers, Harrison had resigned from the Army in 1798 and become the governor of Indiana Territory in 1800. As governor, he had negotiated treaties with the American Indians that acquired millions of acres of land for the United States. His actions had brought him into conflict with the Shawnee brothers Tenskwatawa (the Prophet) and Tecumseh, who were trying to form an American Indian confederacy to oppose further white expansion. In November 1811, Governor Harrison had defeated Tenskwatawa near the American Indian settlement of Prophetstown on the Tippecanoe River.

Shawnee tribe

Embodied most famously in the person of their warrior chief, Tecumseh, the Shawnee tribe played a central role in the War of 1812, fighting in alliance with the British forces and Canadian militia against the United States. The Shawnee were an Algonquian-speaking people hailing from the central Ohio River valley, although they were subsequently displaced by the expansion of the Haudenosaunee (Iroquois) tribe and of the white settlers. Shawnee society was built around often sizeable villages and seasonal hunting camps, subsistence coming from a mix of hunting, fishing, and agriculture, the latter focused on maize and vegetables. They were also, of necessity, a warlike culture, valuing the qualities of bravery and skill in battle.

During the 1760s and 1770s, the Shawnee periodically fought the British settlers, but following the American Revolution they were heavily defeated by the United States at the battle of Fallen Timbers on August 20, 1794. During the War of 1812, Tecumseh brought together a confederacy of American Indian tribes to resist colonial expansion in the Ohio valley, but this effort ended with his defeat and death in October 1813. After this landmark event, the Shawnee split into different branches and dispersed.

The Frontier Besieged

Not knowing that Detroit had already fallen, in late August 1812 Harrison, who was a major general of Kentucky militia, persuaded the senior officer of federal forces in the region, the elderly and uninspiring Brigadier General James Winchester, to permit him to take Colonel Samuel Wells's 17th U.S. Infantry along with three regiments of Kentucky militia to relieve Hull at Detroit. As Harrison explained to Secretary Eustis, "It appeared to me Sir, that it was necessary that someone should undertake the general direction of affairs here and I have done it." Upon learning of Captain Rhea's predicament, Harrison changed course and marched for Fort Wayne. He arrived there with twenty-six hundred men on September 12 but found that the American Indians had already lifted the siege on learning of his approach. He then ordered retaliatory attacks against the American Indians and was in the process of destroying several settlements when General Winchester, whom the president had recently named the commander of the reconstituted Northwestern Army, arrived at Fort Wayne to assume command. The arrangement was short-lived, for on September 24 Harrison received a message from the president appointing him as the commander of the Northwestern Army instead of Winchester. Political pressure from Kentucky, the state that was the strongest supporter of the war, compelled Madison's decision. The new orders gave Harrison, whom Madison had also made a federal brigadier general, command of all the regulars and militia in the theater, almost ten thousand men in total.

▼ William Henry Harrison, by Rembrandt Peale. (National Portrait Gallery, Smithsonian)

Raising a new Northwestern Army severely strained the government's resources, but Eustis gave Harrison full authority to requisition supplies and men. Harrison concluded that regaining Detroit was "considered so important that expense was to be disregarded." He thus freely expended the money, supplies, and resources he thought necessary to accomplish the mission. His objectives were to provide protection for the entire northwestern frontier (stretching from Ohio to the Mississippi River), recapture Detroit, and move against Upper Canada.

Harrison planned to concentrate over four thousand troops at the Maumee River Rapids and, after gathering a million rations there, to

49

advance to Detroit. He would use three converging columns. General Winchester would lead the left wing, composed of the 17th U.S. Infantry, a detachment of the 19th U.S. Infantry, and four Kentucky regiments, based initially at Fort Defiance, Ohio, on the Maumee River. Brigadier General Edward Tupper would command twelve hundred Ohio militia along with some Kentucky mounted riflemen to form the center wing, which would advance along the road Hull's army had cut through the wilderness. Harrison would directly command the right wing, which consisted of a brigade each of Virginia, Ohio, and Pennsylvania militia; the 2d Light Dragoons; and the rest of the 19th U.S. Infantry commanded by Lieutenant Colonel John B. Campbell. In addition, Harrison would assemble as much artillery as possible, eventually accumulating twenty-eight pieces at his headquarters located at Upper Sandusky, Ohio.

Almost half of Harrison's troops were drawn from Kentucky, where there was overwhelming support for the war. Representative Henry Clay expressed the view of his state's citizens to Congress: "I verily believe, that the militia of Kentucky are alone competent to place Montreal and Upper Canada at your feet." Even though he favored using Kentucky militia, Harrison was not oblivious to their lack of discipline. He won the respect and confidence of the militia by explaining rather than dictating orders, in contrast to Winchester whom the Kentuckians intensely disliked.

The effort to obtain sufficient supplies proved to be an extremely challenging task in the sparsely settled region. Harrison organized three main supply routes to support his advance to the Maumee River Rapids. He directed forts be built along each route to serve as magazines for the transfer and storage of provisions and equipment. The left supply route supported Winchester's column and used both land and water transportation from Dayton, Ohio, via Piqua, St. Mary's, and Fort Amanda, to Fort Defiance, since renamed Fort Winchester, Ohio. The center route used Hull's old road from Dayton via Urbana, Fort McArthur, and Fort Findlay to Fort Meigs. The right route went from Franklinton (in present-day Columbus, Ohio) via Delaware, Norton, and Upper Sandusky to Fort Seneca, and Lower Sandusky to Fort Meigs. Harrison asked Eustis for $1 million to cover the expense of moving supplies (see Map 2).

A major problem was the lack of coordination among the various supply agencies. In addition to a commissary agent, Harrison had a quartermaster general and two civilian contractors to furnish commodities: one for troops south of the 41st Parallel and one for forces north of the 41st Parallel. In addition, the commissary department was disorganized and had bad credit with contractors, who required all payments to be made in hard currency. Harrison placed the blame on the "imbecility and incompetence of the public agents and the villainy of the contractors" for the delay in procuring rations.

▲ A heavy cannon overlooks the confluence of the Auglaize and Maumee Rivers, framing the scene at Fort Defiance, Ohio. This particular fort was actually abandoned in 1796, replaced by nearby Fort Winchester. (Wmrapids/CC0 1.0, via Wikimedia Commons)

To provide subsistence, Eustis directed Ebenezer Denny, a Pittsburgh supply contractor, to purchase 1,098,000 rations for Harrison's army. But Harrison believed rations could be procured more economically in southern Ohio and instructed Denny to purchase no more than 400,000. Harrison also asked James White, the contractor south of the 41st Parallel, to build magazines and collect rations at Urbana and Wooster, Ohio. He appointed John H. Piatt as a deputy commissary and directed him to transport 300,000 rations to Fort Defiance, deposit 200,000 rations of flour and 500,000 of beef at Urbana, and purchase and store 500,000 rations at Wooster. When Denny could not procure flour in Pennsylvania, he went to Chillicothe, Ohio, which was in Piatt's territory. Employing the various purchasing agents resulted in competition for scarce resources, and once Harrison realized the confusion he had caused, he redirected Denny to provide for rations as originally ordered by Eustis.

By the end of 1812 and despite enormous expenditure of effort and money, the Northwestern Army was poorly clothed, inadequately fed, and short of all supplies. Winchester's column especially suffered since it had been organized in September, and the troops had no winter clothing. On December 10, Winchester's force ran out of flour, and exposure to the cold caused men to suffer sickness, fever, and

51

Profile:
Soldiers' equipment

The soldiers of the War of 1812 were truly beasts of burden. In an era of literal horsepower, horses and mules were reserved for pulling heavy logistics, while the foot soldiers carried everything else. During this age, one British sergeant of the fusiliers calculated that the total weight carried by an individual soldier was around fifty-nine pounds. This not only included the musket, cartridges, and associated kit (standard ammunition provision was sixty cartridges in a leather cartridge box), but also clothing, knapsack, pipe clay, tent pegs, three days' provisions, water canteen, and (for NCOs) ink, pen, and paper.

U.S. soldiers were similarly loaded, although there was much variation in the volume and type of kit carried depending on the differences between regular army and militia units, and on the erratic logistics of the theater. The American soldier would have his clothing and personal effects in an issue knapsack. Clothing would include extra shirts, trousers, socks, a fatigue blouse, and a fatigue cap, plus a blanket for sleeping. Personal effects were relatively humble. Standard-issue items were typically a shaving kit (razor, shaving brush, shaving soap, and shaving bowl), a simple sewing kit for repairing damage to the uniform or replacing lost buttons, and a comb. A deck of playing cards was also standard and some troops might receive a writing pen and ink. Luxuries were few and far between, not least because the soldier was aware he would have to carry any additional weight across long distances and difficult terrain.

◀ A museum display of the typical personal effects of a U.S. soldier during the War of 1812. Apart from a pipe and a pack of playing cards, personal kit would mostly be focused on sanitation. (DVIDS/Petty Officer 2nd Class Walter Shinn, U.S. Coast Guard)

The Frontier Besieged

frostbite. Over one hundred men perished from disease and about three hundred were constantly sick. Winchester's camp along the Maumee River was described as "Fort Starvation," and one private wrote on Christmas Eve: "Our sufferings at this place have been greater than if we had been in a severe battle … The camp has become a loathsome place." Ammunition supply was so critical that when soldiers

▶ A rear view of a still-working cannon at Fort Malden in Amherstburg, Ontario. Linstock and rammer tools are located beneath the carriage. (ID 97624830 © Roman Halanski/Dreamstime.com)

▼ A plan of Fort Meigs, Perrysburg, Ohio, created by Joseph H. Larwill from a survey conducted on July 19, 1813. Fort Meigs served as a strategic fortification on the Maumee River during the War of 1812, and was the site of two British sieges in 1813. (Toledo-Lucas County Public Library)

The Campaign of 1812

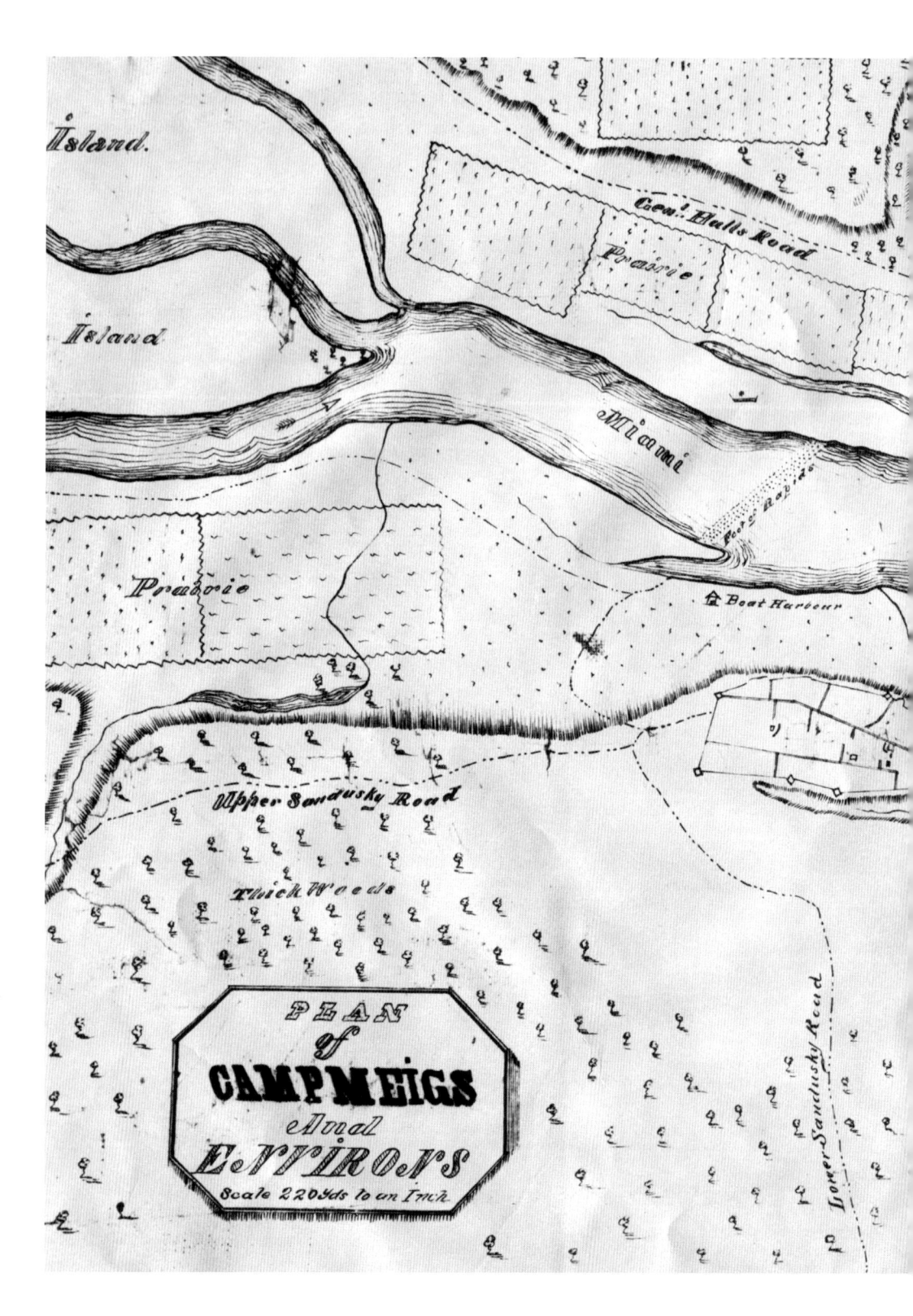

The Frontier Besieged

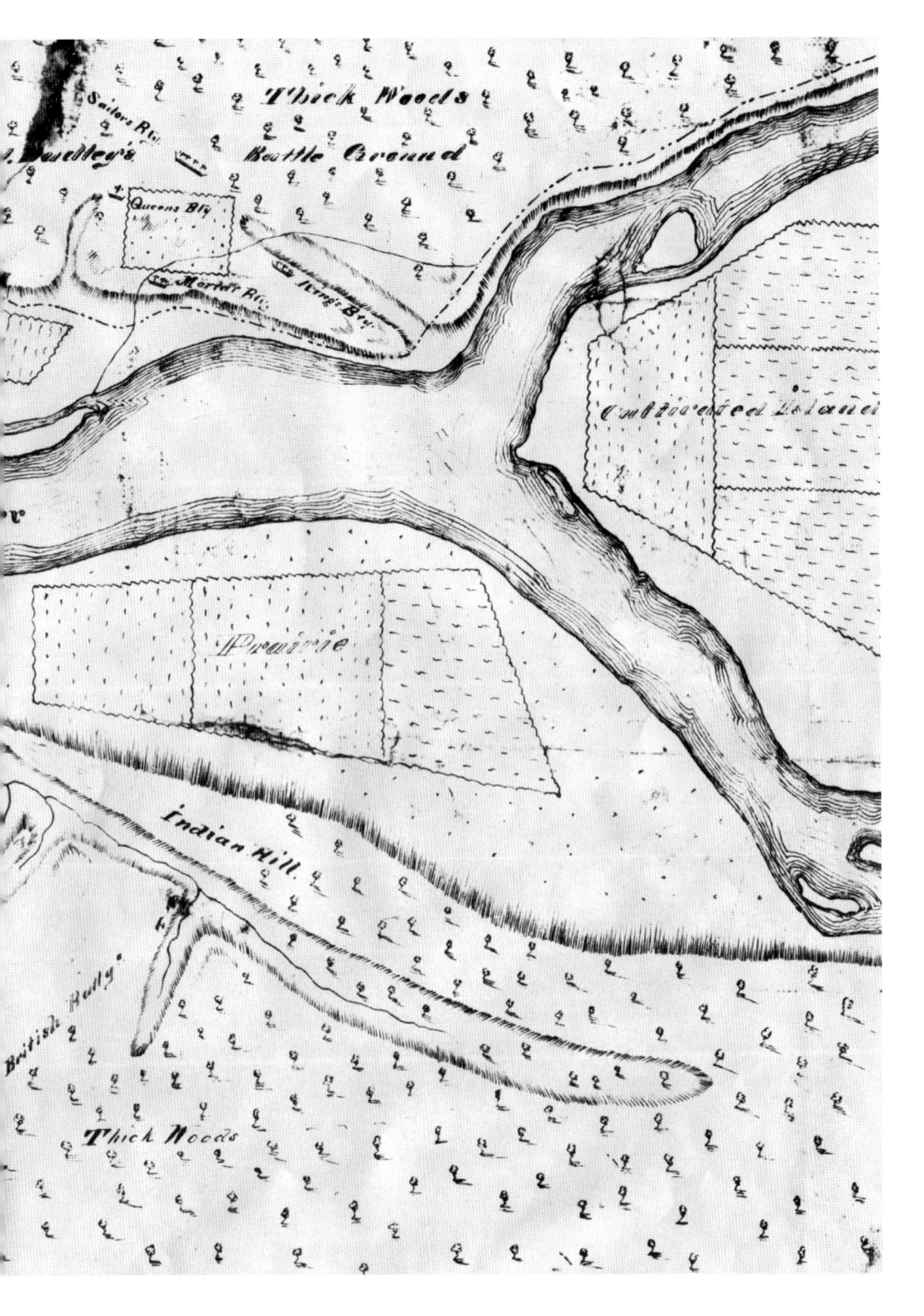

died, no volleys were fired to render military honors at funerals. The effect the winter weather had on operations was evident when General Winchester tried to move his force to the Maumee River Rapids on December 30. The column proceeded slowly, pulling baggage on sleds through snow almost two feet deep. Because of the weakened condition of the men, it took eleven days to march forty miles. This was the state of affairs at the end of December 1812, despite the great exertions by Harrison and his quartermasters to provide supplies.

Hardships notwithstanding, Harrison still managed to inflict suffering on the enemy. On December 17, a column of Kentucky cavalry, militia, and regulars from the 19th Infantry led by Colonel Campbell moved through deep snow in frigid weather to attack and burn a Miami town on the Mississinewa River in Indiana Territory. At dawn the next day, Miami warriors attacked the American encampment. While the regulars held the camp perimeter, the Kentucky cavalry charged and dispersed the attackers. The Americans lost eight killed and forty-eight wounded in the battle of Mississinewa, but the expedition successfully checked the Miamis from making further attacks on American frontier settlements for the remainder of the winter.

▲ A reenactor, dressed as a British soldier, demonstrates firing a musket. Even with careful loading, good-quality ammunition, and steady weapon handling, maximum effective range was usually sub 100 yards. (ID 42274257 © Smontgom65/ Dreamstime.com)

Disaster at the River Raisin

While Harrison's columns were struggling forward through December snow, back in Washington, D.C., William Eustis resigned as secretary of war. James Monroe, the secretary of state, assumed temporary control of the War Department until another Revolutionary War veteran, John Armstrong, took over the position in January 1813.

In correspondence to Harrison, Monroe expressed concern about the upcoming expiration of militia enlistments in February and March 1813 and suggested that further offensive military operations be postponed until spring. Harrison replied that despite the problems of supply, weather, and terrain, he still intended to begin his offensive at the end of January. He planned to make a feint toward Detroit, cross his army over the frozen Detroit River, and attack Fort Amherstburg.

Meanwhile, Winchester managed to get his thirteen hundred men to the Maumee River Rapids on January 10. Two days later, he received news from Frenchtown that the British were harassing the residents and threatening to destroy the village. The British force at Frenchtown consisted of fifty militiamen, about two hundred American Indians, and a 3-pounder manned by regular artillerists. Even though Harrison had ordered him not to advance beyond the rapids, Winchester decided to take action. On January 17, Winchester directed Lieutenant Colonel William Lewis with over six hundred men to advance to Frenchtown, engage the British, and capture any supplies.

Lewis's troops marched thirty-five miles north of the rapids along Hull's old road and across the ice of Lake Erie to reach Frenchtown on the afternoon of January 18. The British detected the Americans as they approached the village and fired on them with artillery.

Lewis ordered his men to charge the enemy position, and after three hours of fighting, the British retreated north into the woods beyond Frenchtown.

Lewis's force not only liberated the small village, but also captured thirty barrels of flour, two thousand pounds of beef, and a large amount of wheat. The Americans lost twelve killed and fifty-five wounded in the engagement. The British admitted losing four dead, but the Americans claimed fifteen enemies killed or captured, most of them American Indians.

Lewis reported the victory to Winchester, who led reinforcements to Frenchtown on January 20, bringing the total U.S. force there to 934 men. The force included 230 men of Colonel Wells's 17th Infantry. Even though it was a regular regiment, it had been in service only since August and was no more experienced than the militia. The rest of the force at Frenchtown consisted of 550 men from the 5th Kentucky Volunteer Regiment led by Colonel Lewis; the 1st Kentucky Rifle Regiment of 100 men led by Lieutenant Colonel John Allen; the 1st Kentucky Volunteer Regiment led by Major Richard M. Gano; a company of rangers led by Captain Henry James; and a troop of light dragoon volunteers led by Captain William Garrard. Although Winchester had advanced to Frenchtown against orders, once there Harrison believed that the position had to be held, and he began efforts to reinforce Winchester.

Convinced that the British would not counterattack, Winchester deployed his troops in exposed positions with their backs to the River Raisin, failed to distribute ammunition, and did not deploy pickets to warn of an enemy approach. He positioned his troops just north of the river, with the Kentucky militia occupying enclosed gardens facing north in a rough semicircle. He positioned the 17th Infantry in an open field one hundred yards to the right of

Exploding shell and shrapnel shell

While much artillery ammunition of the War of 1812 launched inert projectiles—e.g. round shot and grapeshot—there were further types that delivered more explosive impacts on target. One of these was the exploding shell or "common shell." It was produced as what was, in effect, a round shot with a hollow internal cavity, which was filled with a gunpowder charge. The aperture through which the powder was poured was then sealed with a plug. The plug included a fuse that was lit by the heat and flame emitted when the gun was fired. The length of the fuse dictated the amount of time that would pass before the shell exploded; it required a gun crew with experience and judgement to match fuse length with the right moment of detonation, ideally just above the heads of the enemy.

Exploding shells could be unpredictable to use, and were therefore largely applied to land warfare, although the War of 1812 also saw them fired from bomb vessels. Another significant type of exploding shell was the "shrapnel" shell, invented from 1783 by the British Army's then-Lieutenant Henry Shrapnel. The shrapnel shell worked like the exploding shell, but its outer wall was thinner and its gunpowder was mixed with large numbers of musket balls or similar projectiles. (It was essentially a combination of the exploding shell and canister round.) If the shrapnel shell exploded above the enemy, it delivered a devastating combined blast of flame and shot. It was adopted by the British in 1803 and its principles were soon copied by other nations.

Disaster at the River Raisin

the militia, its only protection being a rail fence. Winchester established his headquarters in a house on the south bank of the river, about three-quarters of a mile away. On January 21, Colonel Wells urged General Winchester to deploy scouts and to distribute ammunition to the men. The general ignored Wells's advice and spoke contemptuously of an attack. Wells then sent a message to Harrison about the ill-preparedness of the army stating, "The officers … are truly desirous of seeing you here … Many things ought to be done, which only you know how to do properly."

Meanwhile on January 19, British Colonel Henry Procter crossed the frozen Detroit River from Canada with 597 regulars and militia and about 800 American Indians under the leadership of the Wyandot chief, Roundhead. He also had six artillery pieces that were mounted on sleds. Two hours before dawn on January 22, Procter's army advanced to within musket range of the unsuspecting American troops. His artillery and regulars formed the center, the American Indians were on the right, and the militia and American Indians on his left. A British officer noted the lack of American security and thought the enemy could be taken sleeping in their beds, but as luck would have it, reveille sounded and Winchester's men awoke and observed the approaching British. A Kentucky militiaman, Elias Darnell, recorded in his journal:

> The reveille had not been beating more than two minutes before the sentinels fired three guns in quick succession. The British immediately discharged their artillery, loaded with ball shot, bombs, and grape-shot, which did little injury. The British infantry then charged on those in the pickets, but were repulsed with great loss.

Though surprised by the enemy, the Kentuckians on the left flank concentrated their fire on the British artillery crews and prominent enemy officers. Their marksmanship wreaked havoc among the artillerymen, causing them to abandon some guns. The British regulars attempted to charge the militia's position, but the accurate and deadly fire of the riflemen proved too much for them. The Kentuckians held, but the 17th Infantry was exposed to murderous artillery and musket fire on the open right flank. Twenty minutes after the start of the battle, the 17th Infantry began to fall back. Winchester arrived, still in his bedclothes, but failed to rally the retreating regulars.

▲ A British infantryman and an officer of the 100th Regiment of Foot, as they would be dressed in the regulation uniform of 1812–14. The officer is handling the 1796 Pattern British Infantry Sword. (PD, via Wikimedia Commons)

▼ Kentucky Militia at the River Raisin, by H. Charles McBarron. (Company of Military Historians)

59

The Campaign of 1812

By this time the American Indians had moved to the flank and rear of the Americans. As the regulars fled across the frozen river, the American Indians formed a trap to prevent their escape. The warriors caught, killed, and scalped hundreds of American soldiers. Only a small group led by Captain Richard Matson managed to escape by removing their shoes so their footprints in the snow would deceive the American Indians. These thirty men were the only regulars to escape capture or death. Chief Roundhead also captured Winchester and Lewis, and turned them over to Procter.

As the American right collapsed, the Kentuckians on the left, now commanded by Major George Madison, repelled three more assaults. After an hour of fighting, the Kentuckians had lost just five killed and forty wounded, while the British had lost about a third of their attacking force. Procter asked Winchester to order the Kentuckians to surrender, promising that he would protect them from American Indian vengeance. When men with a white flag approached Madison's position, the Kentuckians thought the British wanted a truce. The Kentuckians reacted to Winchester's plea to surrender with disgust and indignation. However, with their ammunition almost exhausted, their officers felt they could not resist much longer. Madison agreed to surrender, but only after receiving a promise from

▼ The marker sets the location where Lieutenant Colonel William Lewis crossed the eponymous waterway during the first battle of the River Raisin. Lewis was also captured during the battle. (Notorious4life/PD, via Wikimedia Commons)

Scene at the River Raisin, engraving by Albert Bobbett. (New York Public Library)

Procter that he would protect the prisoners and wounded from the American Indians. Elias Darnell recorded: "We were surprised and mortified. There was scarcely a person that could refrain from shedding tears! Some plead with the officers not to surrender, saying they would rather die on the field!" Commenting on the Americans who had suffered months of famine, sickness, and hardship in the wilderness, a British officer remarked:

> The appearance of the American prisoners captured at Frenchtown was miserable to the last degree. They had the air of men to whom cleanliness was a virtue unknown … scarcely an individual was in possession of a great coat or cloak. They were covered with slouched hats beneath which their long hair fell matted and uncombed over their cheeks. … [This] gave them an air of wildness and savageness.

Concerned that Harrison would appear with reinforcements at any moment, Colonel Procter insisted that his army and the prisoners depart for Canada immediately. The battle had cost the British 24 killed and 158 wounded, which they had to evacuate with limited transportation assets. As a result, Procter had no choice but to leave about 80 of the most severely wounded Americans in some of the local buildings, with a promise to send sleighs or other transport for them as soon as possible. He marched the remaining 495 prisoners to Canada.

The next morning about two hundred American Indians entered Frenchtown in an agitated state and began to plunder the village. They stripped the wounded and killed and scalped those who could not move. The American Indians set several buildings on fire and many Americans perished in the flames. One survivor wrote:

The Campaign of 1812

Between daybreak and sunrise, the Indians were seen approaching the houses sheltering the wounded. Pretty soon they came crowding into the room where we were … the Indians tomahawked Captain Hickman in less than six feet from me … and while standing in the snow eighteen inches deep, the Indians brought Captain Hickman out on the porch, stripped of clothing except a flannel shirt, and tossed him out on the snow … after which he breathed once or twice and expired.

When Harrison learned about the defeat at Frenchtown, he wrote to Secretary Monroe that the advance had been made without his consent and the defeat at Frenchtown was "total and complete." Months of planning and preparation had been dashed by the debacle. With no artillery, his men tired, and facing a substantial British force, General Harrison decided to retreat to the Portage River, about thirty miles from the Maumee River Rapids, where he began fortifying his advance position, accumulating supplies, and reorganizing his army. Disturbed by what he saw in the Northwest, Secretary Armstrong endeavored to correct one of the fundamental errors of American strategy during 1812. Realizing that gaining naval control over Lake Erie was the prerequisite to lasting success in the Northwest, he prohibited Harrison from resuming the offensive until the United States had built a fleet on the lake. To ensure compliance, he prevented Harrison from calling out any more militia and limited the Northwestern Army to no more than seven thousand regulars. He also reduced appropriations for supplies to control what he believed had been Harrison's undue waste of resources. Harrison had no recourse but to comply.

The defeat of Winchester's army at Frenchtown further shocked Americans, particularly those in Kentucky, whose families mourned the loss of their fathers,

◀ A contemporary satirical artwork shows Wyandot chief Roundhead capturing Brigadier General James Winchester at the second battle of the River Raisin on January 22, 1813. Winchester remained a prisoner of the British for more than a year. (S. Knight/PD, via Wikimedia Commons)

▲ Erected in 1904, this memorial declares itself as "Michigan's Tribute to Kentucky," and remembers the soldiers of Kentucky who died during the battle of the River Raisin and its associated massacre on January 22 and 23, 1813. (Notorious4life/PD, via Wikimedia Commons)

sons, and brothers. The disaster dealt yet another blow to the spirit of a nation that had deluded itself into thinking that the war would be quickly won. However, the defeat also raised a new determination to avenge the loss, and the rallying cry of "Remember the River Raisin" would be heard whenever Kentuckians fought the British.

War on the Niagara

Unfortunately for the United States, the armies in the other theaters shared the unhappy experiences of those in the Northwest. On the Niagara frontier, military action would be focused along the thirty-six-mile border formed by the Niagara River, which linked the waters of Lake Erie and Lake Ontario.

Settlements on the river were rooted in close commercial and personal relationships between Canadians and Americans, many of whom were related to one another. Prior to the war, the towns of Queenston, Upper Canada, and Lewiston, New York, were important ports for merchant vessels transiting from Lake Ontario. Both towns sat just below the imposing Niagara escarpment, a

▼ This fine maritime artwork captures the battle between the British frigate HMS *Macedonian I* and the American frigate USS *United States*, on October 25, 1812, off the Canary Islands. The U.S. ship, commanded by Commodore Stephen Decatur, captured its opponent as a prize. (Museum of Fine Arts, Boston)

British Army experience in the Peninsular War

The British Army entered the War of 1812 as one of the most experienced fighting forces in the world. Since 1793, Great Britain had been fighting France and its allies in the Revolutionary and Napoleonic Wars, the theaters of combat stretching from the European epicenter out to Africa, Asia, and the Americas, and across the world's oceans. One of the most grinding land actions, however, was the Peninsular War, a physically and morally brutal campaign fought in Spain and Portugal between 1808 and 1814. This theater significantly tested and refined British tactics, particularly in matters regarding the management of long supply lines, the use of light infantry and skirmishers, counter-guerrilla warfare, cooperating with civilian defense forces, maneuvering in broken and difficult terrain, and conducting joint army–navy operations. A significant number of British regiments that fought in the Peninsular War also fought in North America, bringing their experience to bear. However, the fight for the Iberian Peninsula was a greater priority for many in the British military and civilian leadership compared to the struggle in the United States and Canada, resulting in North American units often being under-resourced.

180-foot cliff marking the farthest point where ships could navigate between Lake Ontario and Lake Erie and where the portage road to bypass Niagara Falls began. If the Americans could capture Queenston, then they would be able to sever the British communications route into western Upper Canada and isolate their victory on the Northwest frontier. More importantly, by seizing Queenston, the Americans could then build up forces there to conduct an overland attack on Fort George (see Map 3).

The War Department designated the mix of regular, volunteer, and militia troops in the region as the Army of the Center. Forty-eight-year-old New York militia Major General Stephen Van Rensselaer III commanded the army. Selected by Governor Daniel D. Tompkins because he was among the richest and most politically powerful men in the state, Van Rensselaer had graduated from Harvard University and had served in the state assembly. Although he had been a longtime member of the New York militia, he had never seen active military service. Interestingly, Van Rensselaer was a member of the Federalist Party and had opposed the war with Great Britain. Believing Van Rensselaer would run for governor in the upcoming election, Tompkins offered him the military command as a way of removing his rival. If Van Rensselaer turned down the offer, he would appear unpatriotic. If he accepted and failed—a high prospect given his lack of military training—he would be disgraced and discredited. If by chance Van Rensselaer emerged victorious, the U.S. government would likely want him to continue in service, which would also keep him out of the pending election. Tompkins took delight in the conundrum in which he had placed Van Rensselaer.

To assist him with his new military duties, Van Rensselaer selected his cousin, Lieutenant Colonel Solomon Van Rensselaer, who had served as a Regular Army officer for about ten years. During his service in Wayne's Legion of the United States, he had been severely wounded during the battle of Fallen Timbers in 1794. Together, the two Van Rensselaers faced daunting challenges. By early October 1812, the Army of the Center had grown to almost six thousand soldiers, half of whom were regulars, but most of whom were not yet well trained or disciplined. Severe shortages of tents and blankets added to the soldiers' discomfort, which along with poor sanitation, incapacitated many men with various illnesses.

Brigadier General Alexander Smyth commanded the regulars in Van Rensselaer's army. He refused to recognize Van Rensselaer as his superior and believed he should command the army. When Smyth arrived in Buffalo, he ignored Van Rensselaer's request for a meeting at Lewiston and in correspondence insisted that any offensive operation originate from his location. This fractured relationship extended down the chain of command, causing undue difficulty for the junior regular and militia officers. The result of these self-inflicted wounds added unnecessary challenges to an already arduous American endeavor.

▲ Stephen Van Rensselaer III had a long career in politics, interspersed with military service. His lackluster command of the Army of the Center in the War of 1812, however, particularly his defeat at Queenston Heights, tarnished his reputation as a combat commander. (National Gallery of Art)

Taking advantage of British control over the waterways, General Brock arrived in the Niagara theater on August 24, a week after his victory at Detroit. Only then did he first hear about the armistice agreement negotiated between Dearborn and Prevost, which had gone into effect on August 9. Brock watched with trepidation throughout September as the American army increased its presence along the Niagara frontier. By early October, the British had only six hundred regulars of the 41st and 49th Foot regiments along with six hundred Canadian militia scattered along the Niagara River at Fort George, Queenston, Chippewa, and Fort Erie. About three hundred Iroquois warriors of the Six Nations, led by John Norton and John Brant, were ready to assist their British allies.

During the armistice, some enterprising U.S. Army and Navy officers seized two British warships, the brigs *Detroit* and *Caledonia*, anchored near Fort Erie. In the early morning on October 9, a joint army–navy force rowed from the American shore and boarded the vessels, intending to sail them back to the port at Black Rock, New York. Alerted by the noise, British shore batteries opened

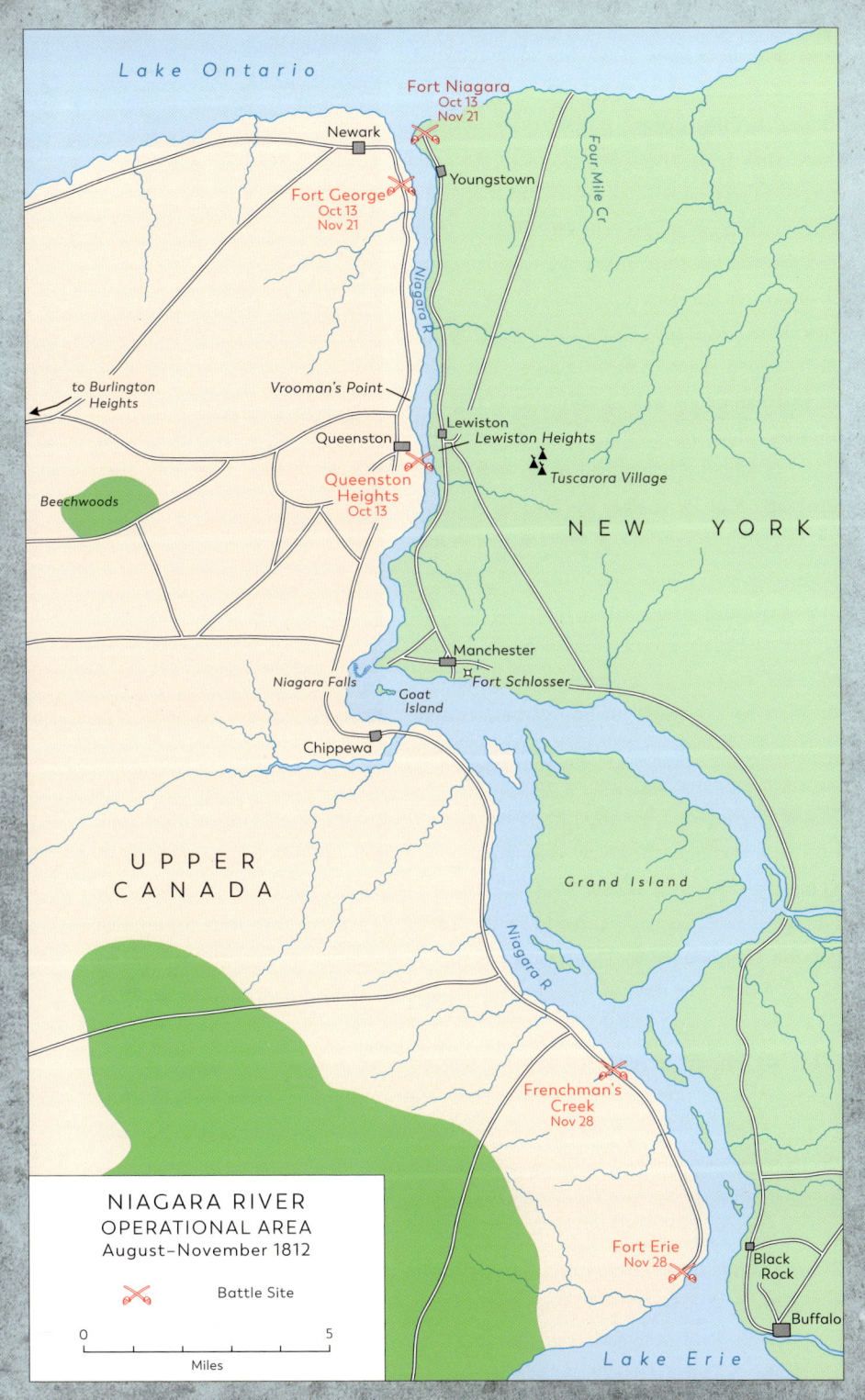

NIAGARA RIVER
OPERATIONAL AREA
August–November 1812

fire. *Detroit* became stuck on Squaw Island, while *Caledonia* maneuvered to the American shore. British troops boarded *Detroit* but were met with effective American fire and forced to retreat. A small American force later burned *Detroit* to prevent the British from recapturing the ship. This bold action seemed to motivate the American militia, which had threatened to return home if something did not happen soon. Believing that "the crisis in this campaign was rapidly advancing and that the blow must soon be struck or all the toil and expense of the campaign will go for nothing," Van Rensselaer decided to conduct an amphibious landing at Queenston. Before finalizing his plans, he wrote to General Smyth at Buffalo suggesting that they meet to coordinate their actions. Smyth never replied to this request. Van Rensselaer therefore decided to use those troops gathered at or near Lewiston to make the invasion. These consisted of two companies from the U.S. Regiment of Riflemen commanded by Major Charles Moseley; the 18th, 19th, and 20th Infantry regiments of New York militia; one company of New York Volunteers commanded by Captain Abraham Dox; five companies of the 13th U.S. Infantry led by Lieutenant Colonel John Chrystie, and two companies from the 2d U.S. Artillery with four 6-pounder cannon commanded by Lieutenant Colonel Winfield Scott. The artillery was to be emplaced on Lewiston Heights to provide covering fire while the infantry crossed the river on boats.

▲ A portrait of Lieutenant General Sir George Prevost, who became known as the "Defender of Canada" for his service during the War of 1812. He held the position of governor general of the Canadas as well as being overall British military commander. (Art Gallery of Nova Scotia/PD, via Wikimedia Commons)

In late afternoon on October 11, the American army assembled at the Lewiston dock, opposite Queenston. New York militia Lieutenant John Simms commanded some experienced rivermen who were to crew the boats to be used for the crossing. Simms, however, drifted past the embarkation point, anchored his boat at the shore, and was never seen again. Some of the other boats arrived at the right place, but most of their oars had been in the boat commanded by Simms. While the soldiers stood waiting until the oars could be found, a violent storm broke. A cold driving rain lasted over twenty-four hours and rendered the flintlock muskets useless, thus postponing the invasion until the night of October 12/13, 1812. During the delay, Van Rensselaer finally received a message from Smyth informing him that Smyth's soldiers would be receiving new uniforms on the thirteenth, and that they needed time to clean up their camp from the effects of the storm, so that they could not participate in the upcoming attack. Smyth would remain at Black Rock with two militia regiments and over one thousand men from five different regular infantry regiments, while Van Rensselaer undertook the invasion of Canada.

Brock had observed the American preparations and believed that the impending attack on Queenston was a feint to divert British attention from the real target, Fort George. The abortive American attempt to cross the river on October 11 affirmed his opinion, especially since it occurred in full view of British positions at Queenston. Brock therefore decided to deploy only two companies of regulars—about one hundred fifty men of the 49th Regiment of Foot—and about one hundred fifty Canadian militiamen at Queenston. They supported one 18-pounder cannon located behind a stone embrasure halfway up the heights, known as the redan battery, and another battery, with two 24-pounder cannon, at Vrooman's Point. Brock kept his main forces near Fort George, where he believed the real American attack would take place.

During the early morning of October 13, three hundred regulars of the 13th U.S. Infantry commanded by Chrystie and three hundred men of the 19th New York militia led by Colonel Van Rensselaer quietly embarked into thirteen waiting boats. At

▼ Field artillery pieces on display at Fort George, Niagara-on-the-Lake. The gun on the right has studded wheel rims to improve traction over rough or muddy ground. (Robert Linsdell/CC BY-SA 2.0, via Wikimedia Commons)

about 0300, as this force neared the Canadian shore, a sentry spotted them and fired, alerting the British garrison at Queenston. Soon the soldiers of the 49th Regiment of Foot stood on the edge of the riverbank rapidly firing their muskets down on the Americans. The Canadian militia joined the battle along with a 9-pounder artillery piece. However, U.S. artillery on Lewiston Heights directed effective counterbattery fire at the British guns. Soldiers recalled a terrible night filled with the noise of gunfire, the thunder of cannon, and the screams of the wounded.

Colonel Van Rensselaer and his boat were almost the last to land on the narrow, rocky shore and were quickly shot to pieces by British musket fire. In a few minutes, nine American officers were wounded, including Van Rensselaer who was hit by six musket balls in his thigh, calves, and heel, soaking his white trousers red with blood. He sought to find Chrystie to have him take over command, but Chrystie had never made it ashore; his boat had broken an oarlock and had drifted past the landing point before returning to Lewiston.

Captain John E. Wool of the 13th U.S. Infantry assumed command of the attack. Though wounded in both hips, he gathered about one hundred fifty men and climbed the heights using a narrow, one-man-wide fisherman's path. The British had left the route unguarded as they did not think it was a feasible approach up the cliffs. But it was, and Wool and his collection of regulars from the 6th, 13th, and 23d U.S. Infantry regiments emerged at a point above the redan battery. When about sixty Americans made it to the top of the hill, Wool led them in a

▲ U.S. Army soldiers during the War of 1812. Although infantry uniforms had a regulation dark-blue color, the scarcity of clothing dyes during the war years meant that the uniforms were often rendered in a drab gray. (*Regular Army Uniforms, The War of 1812*, 1905, by Moffat, Yard & Co.)

charge on the surprised British gunners. Wool's action silenced the battery and enabled the Americans to fire on the British southern flank, while additional troops continued to cross the river from Lewiston.

At Fort George, General Brock heard the artillery fire from the direction of Queenston and mounted his horse to investigate the situation. He left orders for his second in command, Major General Roger Hale Sheaffe, to keep the soldiers at Fort George on alert for any signs of American movement on the other side of the river. Almost an hour later, Brock arrived at Queenston just as dawn began to illuminate the smoke-engulfed town. Simultaneously, more Americans attempted to land, this time north of Queenston at Hamilton Cove, where they were met with severe fire much as their comrades had farther south. One American boat received a direct hit with canister from a British battery that instantly killed or wounded fifteen men.

Brock quickly assessed the situation and determined that the British would have to recapture the redan battery before Wool's contingent could be reinforced. He rallied about fifty regulars and militia, dismounted from his horse, drew his sword, and led his men up the slope to retake the redan. Wool, still bleeding from his wounds, had deployed his men in a defensive circle around the position and was closely watching for an enemy assault. As Brock neared the redan, he raised his sword and turned to urge his men forward, when an American regular leveled his musket and fired a load of buck and ball into the tall British general. Brock, hit in the left side of the chest, fell and died almost immediately.

The prospects for an American victory looked assured. By late morning, the Americans had landed about thirteen hundred men and a

The purchase system

The purchase of officer commissions was an enduring fact of life in the British Army for more than two centuries, from 1661 to 1871. Across this period as a whole, about two-thirds of commissions were bought, the individual paying a sum of money to directly to the person whose post he wished to hold. This meant, naturally, that soldiers from wealthy backgrounds would dominate the officer ranks. The cost of a promotion predictably varied according to the desired rank, hence a young man who had just cleared his sixteenth birthday could buy the rank of ensign in a foot regiment for £400, while a lieutenant colonelcy in the Life Guards might reach £5,200.

But wartime conditions changed matters profoundly. Officer commissions could, and were, obtained through merit and by seniority, the latter referring to an officer stepping into the command gap left when a senior leader was killed. In times of war, as prevailed between 1793 and 1815, the churn of officers through combat losses and the requirements of battlefield competence meant that there were many opportunities to advance without purchase, including through valor, a fact that could encourage the most extreme acts of bravery in the effort to get noticed. In fact, during the war years purchased commissions dropped to about 20 percent of the whole.

The Campaign of 1812

Death of General Brock at Queenston Heights, by John David Kelly. (Library and Archives Canada)

War on the Niagara

The Campaign of 1812

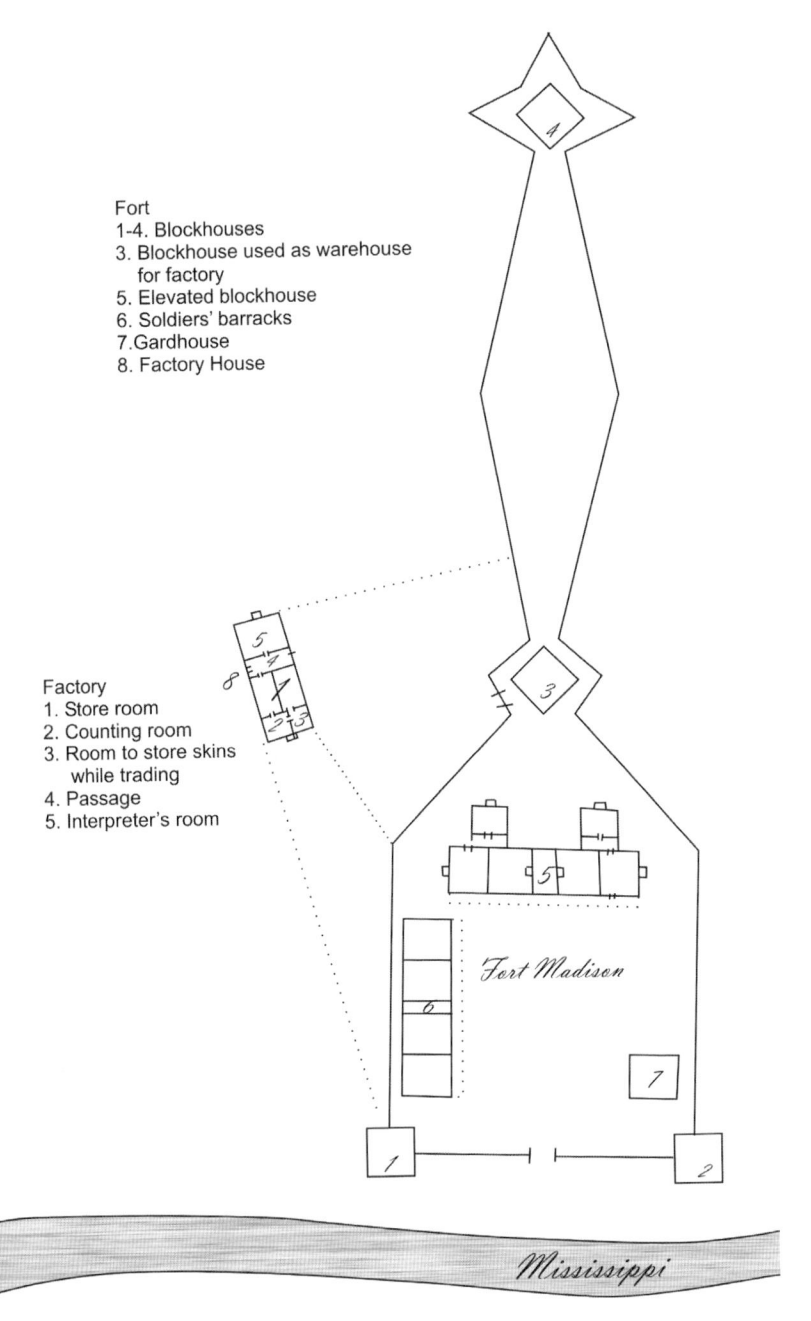

Fort
1-4. Blockhouses
3. Blockhouse used as warehouse for factory
5. Elevated blockhouse
6. Soldiers' barracks
7. Gardhouse
8. Factory House

Factory
1. Store room
2. Counting room
3. Room to store skins while trading
4. Passage
5. Interpreter's room

◄ An 1810 map of Fort Madison, Iowa, illustrates some the defensive and layout considerations and the typical facilities that went into a U.S. military fortification prior to the outbreak of war in 1812. (PD, via Wikimedia Commons)

6-pounder gun. Van Rensselaer, Wool, and other wounded officers had been evacuated back to Lewiston. Finding chaos and confusion, Chrystie, who had finally arrived at about 0700, and Scott went forward to bring order to the operation.

Meanwhile, at about 0400, the American gunners at Fort Niagara had opened an artillery cannonade against Fort George as a diversion. They fired hot shot, which set fire to several buildings in the British fort and nearby town. However, there did not appear to be any activity indicating an assault would be forthcoming, so Sheaffe concluded that the capture of Queenston was the main U.S. objective. Receiving word that Brock had been killed, Sheaffe ordered all available men to march to Queenston, leaving a small garrison at Fort George to continue the artillery duel with Fort Niagara.

About one hundred sixty American Indians of the Six Nations led by John Norton along with some Canadian militiamen had already rushed to Queenston and found the Americans improving their defenses on the heights. After scaling the escarpment, about eighty American Indians occupied the woods at the summit of Queenston Heights and opened a steady fire on the Americans. Though the Americans had about six hundred men in this sector of the battlefield, they had suffered many wounded, were almost out of ammunition, and were in need of food and water and, more importantly, fresh men to renew the attack.

At about 1000, General Van Rensselaer decided to cross the river with as many of the over four thousand troops still at Lewiston as he could. As at Detroit, however, many of the militiamen refused to leave American soil. Reinforcing their doubts over the constitutionality of the matter were fears stoked by the war whoops of Norton's American Indians and the sight of the boats returning from Canada soaked in blood. Van Rensselaer ordered, begged, and pleaded with

▼ Reenactors of the Fort York Guard here show the classic uniforms of the British "Redcoats." Under campaign conditions, of course, such uniforms would deteriorate considerably, with dyes fading, braids fraying, and dirt deeply embedded in the fabric. (Alex L/CC BY-SA 2.0, via Wikimedia Commons)

the militia to help their fellow Americans across the river, but most refused. He stated in his report of the battle, "I rode in all directions; urged the men by every consideration to pass over, but in vain."

Back across the river, as no one could locate Colonel Chrystie, Scott led the action as the men built hasty defenses on top of the heights, skirmished with the American Indians, and awaited badly needed reinforcements. Though Scott did not have a formal military education, he had served in the militia before being commissioned a regular artillery officer in 1808. He was also a voracious reader who had studied important military manuals. His great height, six foot five inches, helped him stand out, and he would prove to be one of the U.S. Army's most gifted tactical commanders during the War of 1812. He had at his disposal 125 regular infantry, 14 regular artillerymen, and 296 militiamen who faced the situation with fortitude and the hope that their comrades at Lewiston would soon come to their aid.

Just after 1300, Sheaffe and his men arrived at Vrooman's Point, where he assessed the situation. Sheaffe, like Brock, decided that he needed to recapture the redan on the heights held by the stranded Americans. But unlike Brock, instead of attacking uphill at the American front, he decided to march his men west around Queenston out of range of the American artillery, then come in behind the Americans from the south along the road from Chippewa. Upon reaching the heights, Sheaffe ordered his force of eight to nine hundred regulars, militia, and American Indians, along with four light artillery pieces, into a line a few hundred yards from the American position. At about 1500, he ordered his men to fix bayonets and advance to the sounds of fifes and drums. They halted about one hundred paces from the Americans, leveled their muskets, and fired. With smoke obscuring the battlefield, the British closed with a fierce bayonet charge punctuated by the war whoops of the American Indians. The panicked Americans had nowhere to retreat with the steep slope of the escarpment and the Niagara River to their rear. Some U.S. soldiers died as they tried to scramble down the escarpment, lost their footing, and fell to their deaths. Others drowned trying to swim the Niagara back to Lewiston. Most, however, threw down their arms and surrendered. Scott carried a white flag and was shot at several times before he was taken to Sheaffe, who accepted the surrender and ordered a cease-fire at about 1600.

After the battle ended, the British discovered hundreds of U.S. troops who had never joined the battle hiding below the cliffs. The British captured a total of 436 U.S. regulars and 489 militia. About five hundred Americans had been killed, drowned, or wounded, many from artillery fire at the beginning of the battle. Of almost six thousand U.S. troops at Lewiston, only about sixteen hundred actually crossed the river during the battle. The British suffered twenty killed, eighty-five wounded, and twenty-two taken as prisoners. After the battle, Sheaffe arranged for a three-day armistice with Van Rensselaer to parole and exchange prisoners. He also offered to send his surgeons to the American lines to help with the wounded. On October 16, Brock was honored with a grand funeral ceremony and was buried in one of the bastions at Fort George. During the funeral, the Americans at Fort Niagara fired their artillery in a salute to a respected opponent.

The thirteen-hour battle was closely fought, and though a clear tactical victory for the British, Sheaffe missed the opportunity to exploit the success and achieve a strategic victory by attacking Fort Niagara. In addition, the death of Brock proved an especially significant blow to British morale. Despite the leadership of Solomon Van Rensselaer, John Wool, and Winfield Scott, the U.S. Army had performed poorly. Thus, the second major campaign ended in disaster, much as that along the Northwest frontier. Stephen Van Rensselaer resigned his command on October 20, still stunned at the outcome, stating, "My extreme mortification at surrendering a victory which had been gallantly won and which I had ample force to have retained, and my disgust at the cause which changed triumph into defeat." Command of the Army of the Center passed to General Smyth, one of the main objects of Van Rensselaer's disgust. Unlike Hull, Van Rensselaer would not be subject to court-martial, but Daniel Tompkins would be reelected as governor of New York in the next election.

▼ This fine panoramic artwork depicting the battle of Queenston Heights suggests the chaos that reigned during contested amphibious actions in the age of oar and sail. (RiverBrink Art Museum, via Wikimedia Commons)

The Campaign of 1812

A soldier's wife at Fort Niagara. (Library of Congress)

Smyth began to organize another offensive along the Niagara River. He wrote to Eustis asking for eight thousand men, one hundred thirty boats, additional artillery, and more supplies of all types. Six weeks later, in mid-November, the revitalized Army of the Center had grown to about four thousand men. On November 17, Smyth issued a proclamation to his troops promising to annex Canada and stating that the "rewards and honours await the brave. Infamy and contempt are reserved for cowards." However, when he polled his men about participating in another invasion, he found that the militia still refused to cross into Canada.

On November 21, an artillery duel broke out between Fort George and Fort Niagara. The resulting cannonade lasted over twelve hours and could be heard as far away as Buffalo. During this action, a woman named Betsy (or Mary Elizabeth) Doyle, whose husband had been captured at Queenston, took an active role servicing the artillery pieces at Fort Niagara with hot shot, which was thrown at the enemy "as if it had been a special messenger of her vengeance."

On November 28, Smyth landed several detachments on the Canadian side of the river. Lieutenant Colonel Charles G. Boerstler led troops from the 14th U.S. Infantry to destroy a bridge at Frenchman's Creek to prevent British reinforcements from reaching the area where the main army would land. Colonel William H. Winder led another attack to capture several British batteries opposite Black Rock, which could oppose the landing of the main force. Winder's force captured the artillery batteries, but enemy scouts detected Boerstler's force and warned their superiors, and coordinated artillery fire soon struck his boats as they crossed the river. As this transpired, Smyth vacillated with the main force, at one point ordering twelve hundred men to disembark for dinner while he held a council of war with his officers to determine what to do next. After issuing a demand to the British commander at Fort Erie to surrender, Smyth ordered his army back into camp for the night.

On November 30, Smyth ordered his soldiers to once again load into the boats only to cancel the operation due to a rainstorm. At this point, the men were fed up and chaos ensued in the American camp. Frightened by the mutinous soldiers, Smyth fled from the encampment. He requested permission from Dearborn to take leave to visit his family, from which he never returned, and the Army eventually dropped him from the rolls. By December 1812, U.S. Army operations had ceased along the Niagara frontier, as the armies went into winter quarters and U.S. leaders struggled with the political and military dilemmas created by their flawed strategy.

The Northern Theater

The third, and final, theater of American offensive operations during 1812 was perhaps the most strategically important because it provided the best opportunity to sever the British supply lines to Upper Canada. The operational area formed a triangle with Montreal at its apex in the north. Kingston, Upper Canada, and Sackett's Harbor, New York, both on Lake Ontario, formed the western points of the triangle, while Plattsburgh, New York, marked its southern point.

Due to the wilderness between Plattsburgh and Lake Ontario, the Americans confined their activities to two avenues of approach into Canada: the corridor formed by eastern Lake Ontario and the St. Lawrence River, and the corridor that ran up through Lake Champlain and Plattsburgh. Generals Dearborn and Prevost oversaw American and British forces, respectively, in this potentially decisive theater of war.

The St. Lawrence Front, July 1812–February 1813

The St. Lawrence River and the eastern portion of Lake Ontario provided a natural point of entry into Canada. Much as in the Northwest and Niagara theaters, control of the waterways was vitally important for moving troops and supplies through the sparsely populated frontier. Also as in other theaters, the United States did not have a naval force on the lake until well after the war began. Sackett's Harbor would serve as the main American naval base on Lake Ontario, while Kingston provided the British a similar harbor.

On July 19, New York militia Brigadier General Jacob J. Brown, a former Quaker, schoolteacher, and now a prosperous landowner, repulsed a British raid on Sackett's Harbor in the first significant action of this region in the war. Dubbed the Fighting Quaker, Brown possessed enthusiasm and combativeness, which proved useful in the back-and-forth raids that soon followed along the Lake Ontario–St. Lawrence frontier. Brown enjoyed the luxury of having a company of well-trained regulars from the U.S. Regiment of Riflemen commanded by

The Northern Theater

the "dashing dare-devil from North Carolina," Captain Benjamin Forsyth. Forsyth's green-coated men were armed with the .54-caliber Model 1803 Harpers Ferry Rifle that could hit a target accurately up to three hundred yards away. They quickly gained a reputation as one of the few American units that could consistently defeat the enemy during the early stages of the War of 1812.

Because of persistent supply and ammunition shortages, Brown ordered Forsyth to organize a raid on the British supply depot at Gananoque, Upper Canada (in present-day Ontario), about forty miles from Sackett's Harbor. Forsyth embarked seventy riflemen and thirty-four militiamen on boats, whereupon they glided among the numerous river islands to avoid detection. On the morning of September 21, Forsyth's unit landed unopposed and surprised about a hundred Canadian militiamen

▼ The artist here strives to convey the bloody reality of the British attempt to capture Fort Stephenson, in Sandusky County, Ohio, on August 2, 1813. Although the British had far superior numbers (augmented by American Indian allies), the American defenders repulsed the repeated attacks. (*Ohio Archaeological and Historical Quarterly*, 1887)

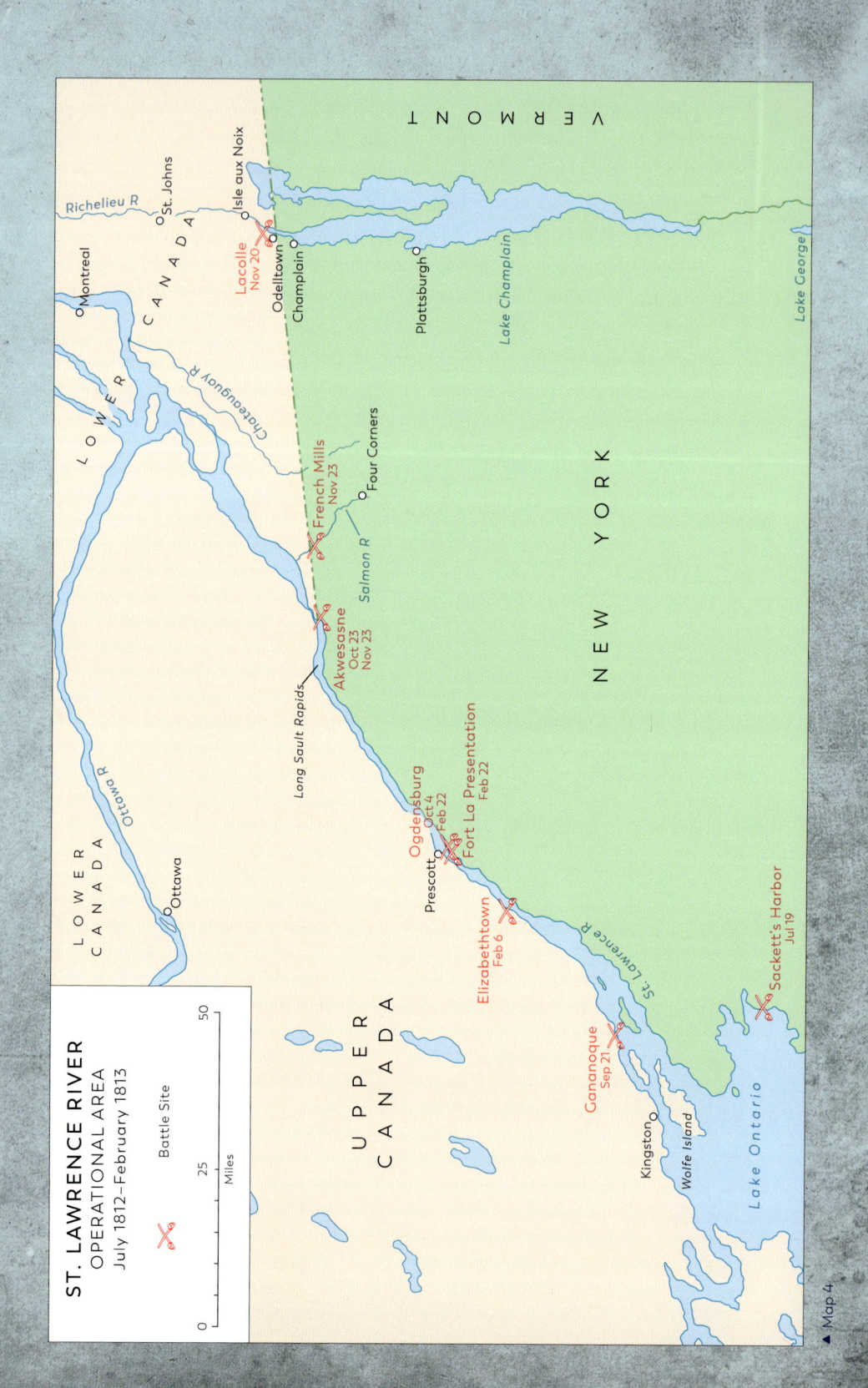

ST. LAWRENCE RIVER
OPERATIONAL AREA
July 1812–February 1813

Battle Site

Map 4

guarding the depot. After forming ranks and exchanging volleys, the American regulars charged, and the militia fled, leaving behind ten dead. The Americans seized dozens of muskets and numerous casks of ammunition, and took eight prisoners. They burned a large storehouse and departed after the thirty-minute action. Forsyth lost one man killed and ten wounded. This daring raid induced the British to strengthen their defenses along the St. Lawrence River, particularly at Kingston, Prescott, and Gananoque (see Map 4).

At the end of September, Brown moved his base of operations from Sackett's Harbor to Ogdensburg, New York, a small village at the confluence of the Oswegatchie and St. Lawrence Rivers, directly opposite Prescott, Upper Canada, and astride the main British supply line to the Great Lakes. Both towns served as transshipment points for commerce bypassing the rapids on the St. Lawrence River. Brown's men garrisoned the village and built several artillery batteries aimed toward Prescott. For this they won few accolades from the largely Federalist citizens of Ogdensburg, who had until that time enjoyed a thriving trade with their friends and relatives living in Canada. Economic and family ties trumped national loyalty.

▲ *Jacob J. Brown, engraving by Thomas Gimbrede. (New York Public Library)*

On October 4, the British launched the first of several operations against Ogdensburg. Disregarding Prevost's nonaggression policy, Colonel Robert Lethbridge organized an amphibious attack. Brown waited until the enemy was halfway across the river, then ordered his batteries to fire, killing three men and wounding nine. The British boats returned to Prescott without reaching the American shore, and Prevost recalled Lethbridge to Montreal when he heard of the fiasco.

On October 23, two hundred New York militia commanded by Major Guilford D. Young departed Troy, New York, to attack Akwesasne, a community of French-Catholic Mohawks located on the St. Lawrence southwest of Montreal at Lake St. Francis and straddled the border. A company of the Corps of Canadian Voltigeurs under the command of Captain John MacDonnell guarded Akwesasne. During the raid, the Americans captured the post, killed seven of the British, and took forty-one prisoners. A small party of New York militia then remained to guard this post.

The Campaign of 1812

The British retaliated in November when British Captain Andrew Gray, who was proceeding up the St. Lawrence River with a convoy of bateaux filled with supplies, received orders to recapture Akwesasne and attack the American post at French Mills, New York, located on the Salmon River about nine miles to the east. Gray gathered a mixed force of regulars and militia and led it across the Salmon River before dawn on November 23. He regained control of Akwesasne without opposition from the squad of Americans stationed there. Upon arrival at French Mills, he surprised and defeated the New York militia garrison, killing three men and capturing forty-two. The British then destroyed any arms, ammunition, and bateaux they could not carry away.

The winter passed quietly in the region until the North Carolina daredevil, the newly promoted Major Forsyth, broke the calm. During the early morning of February 6, 1813, he led two hundred riflemen and militia in sleighs across the frozen St. Lawrence River to liberate Americans imprisoned at Elizabethtown, Upper Canada (present-day Brockville, Canada). The raiders surprised the garrison in their beds and freed the prisoners. They captured fifty-two Canadian militiamen and seized one hundred twenty stands of arms that the British had previously captured at Detroit. They then returned to Ogdensburg having suffered one man wounded. The action earned Forsyth a brevet promotion to

▼ Reenactors at Fort George, Niagara-on-the-Lake, present themselves smartly as British Redcoats on parade. The red jackets would remain a key feature of British Army infantry uniform until the adoption of the khaki service dress in 1902. (ID 33725408 © Florentino David | Dreamstime.com)

lieutenant colonel, and the magazine the *Niles Weekly Register* proclaimed him to be a "terror to the enemy."

The raid proved to be Forsyth's undoing. The British commander at Prescott, Lieutenant Colonel George MacDonnell, had frequently appealed to Prevost for permission to attack Ogdensburg, but to no avail. Unwilling to allow the Elizabethtown raid to go unanswered, on February 22, 1813, Colonel MacDonnell decided to ignore Prevost's orders and assault Ogdensburg. He organized his force of eight hundred men into two columns. The right column, commanded by Captain John Jenkins, was to attack the town near the old French Fort La Presentation on the west bank of the Oswegatchie River. Simultaneously, the left column, which included some artillery and was under MacDonnell's direct command, would attack from the east. Both columns would have to move through heavy snow, which further added to the difficulty of this maneuver.

The American defenders consisted of Forsyth's rifle company and four understrength companies of New York militia. MacDonnell's column quickly captured several American batteries on the river, while Jenkins's column ran into stiff opposition at Fort La Presentation, where the riflemen inflicted heavy casualties on the British. During a pause in the action, MacDonnell demanded that Forsyth surrender. Forsyth, however, managed to escape. The British occupied Ogdensburg and burned two large barracks, two merchant vessels, and two gunboats. The British lost seven men killed and sixty-three wounded, including MacDonnell and Jenkins, while the Americans suffered three killed, seventeen wounded, and fifty-two captured.

Forsyth withdrew about nine miles from Ogdensburg and sent a message to Colonel Alexander Macomb at Sackett's Harbor, asking for three hundred reinforcements to mount a counterattack to regain Ogdensburg and to seize Prescott. Macomb would send no reinforcements, so Forsyth and his command moved to Sackett's Harbor. Thereafter the citizens of Ogdensburg refused to allow American troops to return to the town, fearing their presence would lead to further bloodshed and destruction. For the remainder of the war, the British supply convoys would pass this stretch of the St. Lawrence River unmolested.

The Plattsburgh Front, November–December 1812

While the warring parties sparred along the St. Lawrence frontier, General Dearborn planned to strike a knockout blow against the heart of British administration in Canada, the city of Montreal, via Plattsburgh. To execute the mission, in early September he formed what he called the Northern Army. By November 8, over one thousand troops had arrived. Dearborn, however, dithered, and he did not arrive at Plattsburgh until November 10, where he found an army weakened by illness and lax discipline. Finally, in

The Campaign of 1812

mid-November, he decided to undertake the long-awaited offensive to seize Montreal. But the delay would prove costly. Not only had cold weather and inclement conditions set in that would adversely affect operations, but also the other two prongs of his grand strategic design had already run their course and ended in failure at Detroit and Queenston. The advance against Montreal would go forward alone.

General Dearborn's army numbered about six thousand men, including seven regiments of regular infantry, some artillery, and light dragoons. In addition, he had a variety of militia from various northeastern states. The commanding general divided this force into two brigades: one commanded by Brigadier General Joseph Bloomfield and the other by Brigadier General John Chandler. Dearborn wanted Bloomfield to lead the offensive, but when he became ill, Dearborn reluctantly chose to lead it himself. On November 19, the Americans reached Champlain, New York, just below the Canadian border. Here Dearborn faced the same situation that Hull and Van Rensselaer had experienced when about half of his militia refused to cross the Canadian border.

Early on November 20, Colonel Zebulon M. Pike crossed into Canada with six hundred fifty men of the 15th U.S. Infantry and three hundred militiamen, and advanced on Lacolle, a small village two miles west of the Richelieu River and five miles north of the New York border. A small contingent of the Canadian Voltigeurs, some fur traders, and Kahnawake Mohawks commanded by Lieutenant Colonel Charles-Michel de Salaberry defended the town.

Pike formed his men on line and ordered them to attack only with bayonets. The British put up a brief defense at a blockhouse but were forced to retreat. The Americans proceeded to destroy many of the buildings of the village as darkness fell. However, the small victory was soon spoiled. Some Americans accidentally fired on a body of New York militia who had trailed behind the main force and were mistaken for Canadians. A confused, two-hour firefight ensued that left two Americans dead, twelve wounded, and five missing. Meanwhile, de Salaberry returned to Lacolle with about one hundred Voltigeurs and two hundred thirty Kahnawake warriors. This proved too much for the Americans who withdrew back to Champlain.

◀ This 1895 illustration depicts the death of a soldier of the Glengarry Light Infantry during the British attack across the frozen St. Lawrence River during the battle of Ogdensburg on February 22, 1813. (*Illustrated Battles of the Nineteenth Century*, Volume 2, 1895/ British Library)

At this point, Dearborn called a council of war with his subordinate officers who recommended returning to Plattsburgh and winter quarters. On November 22, the Northern Army began marching south, and the next day the militiamen were discharged and sent home, while the regulars went into winter quarters. Fully expecting to be blamed, or at worst relieved of command, Dearborn was surprised that responsibility for the cumulative disasters fell instead upon Secretary Eustis. On December 3, 1812, Eustis resigned as secretary of war. Both his tenure and the year 1812 had come to an end.

The Campaign of 1812

A blockhouse at Old Fort Niagara overlooks the waters of Lake Ontario. This fortification began the war in American hands, but was captured by the British in December 1813. (ID 340274485 © Randall Runtsch | Dreamstime.com)

The Northern Theater

Analysis

The year 1812 and the early months of 1813 had been bitterly disappointing for the United States Army. The defeat of American arms at Detroit, Queenston Heights, the River Raisin, and Ogdensburg—not to mention Dearborn's failed invasion of Canada—illustrated a systemic institutional failure of leadership, organization, training, and logistics. The United States had simply not prepared for a war it chose to fight.

At its root, the strategic plan for the invasion of Canada proved far beyond the capabilities of the United States Army. The organization and administration of the War Department was wholly inadequate for the task it faced. Eustis demonstrated, and later admitted, that he was unable to cope with the burgeoning responsibilities of war. His focus on petty details instead of the larger problems of leadership and policy greatly hindered the early campaigns. Unreliable and slow overland transportation also hampered communications between Washington and the field commanders. The secretary of war often did not know what decisions or movements his commanders were making, while commanders often waited for clarification of orders or misinterpreted what they were being asked to do. As a result, the Army failed to coordinate operations on the three major theaters.

Logistics, too, proved a critical weakness. The field armies depended on civilian contractors for all classes of supplies and transportation. Under the contract system, rations were purchased, and the contractor had to deliver them in a specific quantity, to a specific place, and at a specific time. Most contractors were unreliable in this regard. Transportation was not only slow, but also added to the cost of supplies. The loss of horses and the expense of forage raised the price the Army paid for a barrel of pork to $127, a barrel of flour to $100, and a bushel of oats to $160. British control of the waterways exacerbated this problem, forcing the Army to move supplies laboriously overland.

Madison's idea of concentrating the Army for a strike north toward Montreal made sense both logistically and strategically, but the local inhabitants were less

▲ The modern-day Fort Malden National Historic Site, Ontario. During the War of 1812 it was a key British stronghold, at least until it was burned and abandoned in September 1813. (Dwight Burdett/CC BY-SA 3.0, via Wikimedia Commons)

than enthusiastic about waging war against their Canadian trading partners. Many New England states argued they were not threatened by invasion from that quarter, but by sea, and so tended to focus their resources on coastal defense. Conversely, it was politically and logistically impossible to convince troops from the West and South, where the war was generally popular, to move to New York and to bear the brunt of offensive operations while New Englanders remained passive.

Another culprit in the nation's failure in 1812 was the militia system. For philosophical, political, and financial reasons, the founders of the nation had chosen a manpower policy that relied on a small standing army in peace and the more numerous, but less well-trained and disciplined, state militias during war. All too frequently in 1812, the nation's militia proved unequal to the task. Moreover, many militiamen felt no obligation to serve outside of their home states and absolutely refused to invade another country. Thus public rhetoric about easily seizing Canada clashed with the reality of actually carrying out the invasion under very unfavorable circumstances.

The enemy also played a role, as should be expected, in thwarting U.S. offensive operations. The British enjoyed the advantage of interior lines of movement, communications, and supply, facilitated by control of the waterways. They were thus able to shift their limited forces from one threatened theater to the next to defeat each of the unsynchronized American threats in turn. Elated by

The Campaign of 1812

◄ At the historic Fort Dearborn in 1932, soldiers and civilians formally mark the 120th anniversary of the massacre at the site in 1812. (The Newberry Library)

their unexpected success, Anglo-Canadian morale soared, further raising the challenge for a demoralized America.

At the tactical level, the U.S. Army clearly needed more than just good generals, although these too had been in short supply in 1812. It badly needed competent junior officers and soldiers who were thoroughly trained and disciplined. Developing such men and fixing the Army's shortcomings in organization, communications, and logistics would take time, and solid leadership. Until these could be found, prospects for victory—so deceptively bright in the heady days following the declaration of war in June 1812—looked dim.

Further Reading

Berton, Pierre. *The Invasion of Canada: 1812–1813*. Toronto: Anchor Canada, 2011.

Campbell, Maria. *Revolutionary Services and Civil Life of General William Hull*. Legare Street Press, 2022.

Crackel, Theodore J. "The Battle of Queenston Heights." In *America's First Battles*. Edited by Charles E. Heller and William A. Stofft. Lawrence: University Press of Kansas, 1986.

Feltoe, Richard. *The Pendulum of War: The Fight for Upper Canada, January–June 1813*. Toronto: Dundurn Press, 2013.

———. *The Pendulum of War: The Fight for Upper Canada, July–December 1813*. Toronto: Dundurn Press, 2013.

Fredrikson, John C. *Green Coats and Glory: The United States Regiment of Riflemen 1808–1821*. Youngstown, N.Y.: Old Fort Niagara Association, 2000.

———. *The United States Army in the War of 1812: Concise Biographies of Commanders and Operational Histories of Regiments, with Bibliographies of Published and Primary Sources*. Jefferson, N.C.: McFarland & Company, 2009.

Hickey, Donald R. *The War of 1812: A Forgotten Conflict*. Urbana: University of Illinois Press, 1989.

Hitsman, J. Mackay. *The Incredible War of 1812*. Rev. ed. Toronto: Robin Brass Studio, 2000.

Kochan, James. *The United States Army 1783–1811*. Oxford: Osprey Publishing, 2001.

Malcomson, Robert. *Lords of the Lake: The Naval War on Lake Ontario, 1812–1814*. Annapolis, MD: Naval Institute Press, 1998.

———. *A Very Brilliant Affair: The Battle of Queenston Heights, 1812*. Annapolis, Md.: Naval Institute Press, 2003.

Muehlbauer, Matthew S. and David J. Ulbrich. *Ways of War: American Military History from the Colonial Era to the Twenty-First Century*. London: Routledge, 2017.

Quimby, Robert S. *The U.S. Army in the War of 1812: An Operational and Command Study*. East Lansing: Michigan State University Press, 1997.

Riley, Jonathan. *A Matter of Honour: The Life, Campaigns and Generalship of Isaac Brock*. Barnsley, UK: Frontline Books, 2011.

Skaggs, David Curtis and Gerard T. Altoff. *A Signal Victory: The Lake Erie Campaign, 1812–1813*. Annapolis, Md.: Naval Institute Press, 1997.

Stagg, J. C. A. *The War of 1812: Conflict for a Continent*. Cambridge, UK: Cambridge University Press, 2012.

Taylor, Alan. *The Civil War of 1812: American Citizens, British Subjects, Irish Rebels, & Indian Allies*. New York: Vintage Books, 2011.

Tucker, Spencer C., ed. *The Encyclopedia of the War of 1812*. 3 vols. Santa Barbara, Calif.: ABC-CLIO, 2012.

Wooster, Robert. *The American Military Frontiers: The United States Army in the West, 1783–1900 (Histories of the American Frontier Series)*. Albuquerque, NM: University of New Mexico Press, 2012.

Index

41st Parallel, 50–51

Akwesasne, 8, 82, 83–84
American Indian tribes
    Fox, 47–48
    Iroquois (or Haudenosaunee), 48, 66
    Miami, 9, 47, 56
    Mohawk, 8, 83, 87
        Kahnawake, 87
    Potawatomi, 7, 43, 47
    Shawnee, 21, 47, 48
    Winnebago, 47–48
    Wyandot, 7, 37, 59, 62
ammunition, 52, 83, 84
    exploding shell (or "common shell"), 58
    grapeshot, 58
    musket ball, 58, 70
    round shot, 58
    shortages of, 17, 48, 53–56, 58, 60, 75, 81
    "shrapnel" shell, 58
Army of the Center (U.S.), 65, 66, 77, 78
artillery
    3-pounder cannon, 57
    6-pounder cannon, 37, 68, 74
    9-pounder cannon, 37, 70
    18-pounder cannon, 69
    24-pounder cannon, 69

batteries, 66–68, 78, 83, 85
battle of
    Fallen Timbers, 21, 48, 66
    Fort Dearborn, 7, 41
    Fort Detroit, 7

    Monguagon, 7, 40
    Queenston Heights, 6, 9, 20, 66, 72, 75, 77, 90
    River Raisin, 9, 57–63
        first battle, 9, 60
        second battle, 9, 62
British forces
    8th (King's) Regiment of Foot, 20
    41st Regiment of Foot, 31, 38, 66
    49th Regiment of Foot, 20, 66, 69, 70
    Glengarry Light Infantry, 86–87
    Royal Newfoundland Infantry Fencibles, 31
British Indian Department, 31
Brock, Maj. Gen. Sir Isaac, 7, 8, 20, 21, 38, 43, 44, 46, 66, 69, 71, 72, 75, 76, 77
Brown, Brig. Gen. Jacob J., 7, 80–81, 83
Brush, Capt. Henry, 37

Caledonia (British warship), 66, 68
Cass, Col. Lewis, 28, 33, 36, 41, 43, 44, 46
cavalry, 9, 28, 56
Chrystie, Lt. Col. John, 68, 69, 70, 74, 76
commissions, 20, 45, 71
Corps of U.S. Artillery, 26
court-martial, 45, 46, 77
Cuyahoga (U.S. unarmed schooner), 31, 32

Dearborn, Maj. Gen. Henry, 8, 15, 17, 18, 23, 25, 40–41, 46, 66, 79, 80, 85–87, 90
deserters/desertion, 10, 33, 36, 44
Detroit, 7, 23, 25, 26–33, 36–38, 40–44, 46, 47, 49–50, 57, 66, 75, 85, 87, 90
Detroit (British warship), 66, 68
dragoons, 13, 16, 50, 87

encampments, 31, 56, 79
Eustis, Secretary of War William, 16, 17, 24, 25, 28, 29, 31, 32, 36, 40, 44, 49, 50, 51, 57, 78, 87, 90

Federalist Party, the, 16, 65
Forsyth, Maj. Benjamin, 81, 83, 84–85
Fort Amherstburg, 27, 31, 32–33, 36, 39, 53, 57
Fort Dearborn, 7, 13, 15, 41, 42, 43, 92
Fort Defiance, 50–51
Fort Detroit, 26, 31–32, 43–44, 45, 46
Fort Erie, 66, 79
Fort George, 65, 66, 69, 71, 74–75, 77, 78, 84
Fort Mackinac, 7, 13, 32, 36–37, 43, 46
Fort Niagara, 73–74, 77, 78, 88
Fort Osage, 13
Fort Wayne, 43, 48, 49
Frenchtown, 9, 31, 37, 38, 57–58, 61–62

General Hunter (British gun brig), 31, 44
Great Lakes, the, 23, 25, 28, 83

Hanks, Lt. Porter, 37
Harrison, Commander of the Northwestern Army William Henry, 7, 40, 47, 48–51, 56, 57, 58, 59, 61, 62
Heald, Capt. Nathan, 41, 43

95

Hull, Brig. Gen. William, 7, 20, 26, 28, 29, 31–33, 36, 37, 38, 40, 41, 43–46, 49, 50, 57, 77, 87

Indiana Territory, 9, 40, 43, 47, 48, 56

Jefferson, President Thomas, 16, 17, 18, 45

Lady Prevost (British schooner), 31

Lake Erie, 26, 28, 57, 62, 64, 65

Lake Michigan, 15, 43

Lake Ontario, 23, 64–65, 80, 88

Legion of the United States, 66

Lewiston, 64, 66, 68, 70, 71, 74, 75, 76–77

Lower Canada, 19, 23, 34

MacDonnell, Lt. Col. George, 9, 83, 85

Mackinac Island, Michigan, 7, 32, 36

Madison, Maj. George, 60

Madison, President James, 10, 12, 16, 18, 23, 28, 40, 45, 46, 49

magazines, 15, 28, 29, 50, 51

Maumee River, 7, 31

 Rapids, 7, 26, 31, 49–50, 51, 56, 57, 62

McArthur, Col. Duncan, 28

Meigs, Governor Return Jonathan, 28, 37, 41

Michigan Territory, 23, 26, 28, 31, 45

Miller, Lt. Col. James, 28, 29, 33, 38, 40

Missouri Territory, 13

Monroe, Secretary of War James, 57, 62

Montreal, 8, 19, 22–23, 50, 80, 83, 85, 87, 90

Niagara-on-the-Lake, 69, 84

Niagara River, 8, 23, 64, 66, 76, 78

Northwestern Army, the, 26, 28–29, 31, 46, 49, 51, 62

Norton, John, 66, 75

Ogdensburg, New York, 8, 9, 83, 85, 86, 90

Ordnance Department, 7, 17

Peninsular War, the, 65

pickets, 15, 58, 59

Pike, Col. Zebulon M., 8, 87

Prevost, Lt. Gen. Sir George, 19, 20, 23, 40, 66, 68, 80, 83, 85

Queen Charlotte (British sloop-of-war), 31, 36, 44

Queenston, Upper Canada, 8, 64, 65, 68, 69–70, 71, 75, 76, 78, 87, 90

rangers, 13, 28, 58

rations, 32, 49, 50–51, 90

reenactors, 29, 75, 84

Republican Party, the, 16, 17

Rhea, Capt. James, 48, 49

Roberts, Capt. Charles, 37

Roundhead (American Indian chief), 59, 60, 62

Sackett's Harbor, New York, 80, 81, 83, 85

 raid on, 7

scalping, 38, 60, 61

Scott, Lt. Col. Winfield, 18, 68, 74, 76, 77

Sheaffe, Maj. Gen. Roger Hale, 71, 75, 76, 77

Simms, Lt. John, 68

skirmishes/skirmishing, 36, 65, 76

Smyth, Brig. Gen. Alexander, 66, 68–69, 77–79

St. George, Lt. Col. Thomas B., 31, 33

St. Lawrence River, 8, 23, 41, 43, 80, 83, 84, 85, 86

Taylor, Capt. Zachary, 47

Tecumseh, Shawnee leader, 20, 21, 38, 40, 48

Tenskwatawa, "the Prophet," 21, 48

Tompkins, Gov. Daniel D., 65, 77

truces, 40–41, 60

uniform, 14, 16, 17, 52, 59, 68–69, 70, 75, 84

Upper Canada (present-day Ontario), 19, 20–21, 23, 26, 28, 41, 49, 50, 64, 65, 80

U.S. forces

 regiments

  1st Kentucky Rifle Regiment, 58

  1st U.S. Infantry Regiment, 15, 26

  2d Regiment of Light Dragoons, 50

  2d U.S. Artillery Regiment, 68

  4th U.S. Infantry Regiment, 28–29, 33, 38

  5th Kentucky Volunteer Regiment, 58

  6th U.S. Infantry Regiment, 70

  13th U.S. Infantry Regiment, 68, 69–70

  17th U.S. Infantry Regiment, 49, 50, 58–59

  18th Infantry Regiment of New York (militia), 68

  19th Infantry Regiment of New York (militia), 68, 69

  19th U.S. Infantry Regiment, 9, 50, 56

  20th Infantry Regiment of New York (militia), 68

  23d U.S. Infantry Regiment, 70

  U.S. Regiment of Riflemen, 68, 80–81

Van Horne, Maj. Thomas, 38

Van Rensselaer III, Maj. Gen. Stephen, 65–66, 68–70, 74, 75–76, 77, 87

Van Rensselaer, Lt. Col. Solomon, 65–66

War Department, 14, 16, 25, 26, 57, 65, 90

Wayne, Gen. Anthony, 31, 48

weapons, 7, 8, 17, 28, 31

 .54-caliber Model 1803 Harpers Ferry Rifle, 81

 bayonets, 29, 40, 76, 87

 muskets, 43, 52, 56, 59, 68, 70, 71, 83

 swords, 43, 71

  1796 Pattern British Infantry Sword, 59

Wells, Capt. William, 41, 43

Wells, Col. Samuel, 49, 58, 59

West Point (U.S. Military Academy), 16, 18, 43

Whistler, Capt. John, 15, 26

Winchester, Brig. Gen. James, 9, 49, 50, 51, 53, 56, 57, 58–60, 62

Wool, Capt. John E., 70–71, 74, 77

Young, Maj. Guildford D., 8, 83